How to Make Friends

A Step-by-step Guide to Meeting People

(The Most Effective Strategies to Help You Build Friendships, Become More Persuasive)

Paul Goode

Published By **Percy Clint**

Paul Goode

All Rights Reserved

How to Make Friends: A Step-by-step Guide to Meeting People (The Most Effective Strategies to Help You Build Friendships, Become More Persuasive)

ISBN 978-1-7382986-7-9

No part of this guidebook shall be reproduced in any form without permission in writing from the publisher except in the case of brief quotations embodied in critical articles or reviews.

Legal & Disclaimer

The information contained in this book is not designed to replace or take the place of any form of medicine or professional medical advice. The information in this book has been provided for educational & entertainment purposes only.

The information contained in this book has been compiled from sources deemed reliable, and it is accurate to the best of the Author's knowledge; however, the Author cannot guarantee its accuracy and validity and cannot be held liable for any errors or omissions. Changes are periodically made to this book. You must consult your doctor or get professional medical advice before using any of the suggested remedies, techniques, or information in this book.

Upon using the information contained in this book, you agree to hold harmless the Author from and against any damages, costs, and expenses, including any legal fees potentially resulting from the application of any of the information provided by this guide. This disclaimer applies to any damages or injury caused by the use and application, whether directly or indirectly, of any advice or information presented, whether for breach of contract, tort, negligence, personal injury, criminal intent, or under any other cause of action.

You agree to accept all risks of using the information presented inside this book. You need to consult a professional medical practitioner in order to ensure you are both able and healthy enough to participate in this program.

Table Of Contents

Chapter 1: The Essence of Friendship 1

Chapter 2: The Foundation of Friendships 11

Chapter 3: Initiating Meaningful Conversations 28

Chapter 4: Building Lasting Connections. 39

Chapter 5: Resilience in Friendships 57

Chapter 6: Expanding Your Social Horizons 71

Chapter 7: Prioritizing and Investing In Connections 81

Chapter 8: Understanding College Life ... 93

Chapter 9: Finding Your Niche 109

Chapter 10: Effective Communication Skills 125

Chapter 11: Attending Social Events 143

Chapter 12: Online and Virtual Friendships 161

Chapter 13: Maintaining and Nurturing
Friendships 173

Chapter 1: The Essence Of Friendship

Defining True Friendship

It's a hot summer time day on the second day of August, 216 BC, on a dusty discipline near Cannae, southern Italy. The air is thick with the sound of clanging swords and shields, and in case you were there, you'll be capable of perfume the sweat and fear of the infantrymen amassed round. Hannibal Barca, collectively with his pal Maharbal and brother Hasdrubal Barca, lead the Carthaginian forces. The Roman navy is commanded via Consuls Lucius Aemilius Paullus and Gaius Terentius Varro. The Roman navy is arrayed in tight formations, equipped to stand the Carthaginian forces which have been terrorizing the Italian peninsula for years. The armies march closer to every exclusive, and lots of hearts are racing with anticipation.

As the two armies draw nearer, the air is packed with the deafening sound of trumpets and the pounding of drums. The Romans have usual a dense phalanx, with their spears and shields held tightly collectively, at the identical time due to the fact the Carthaginians unfold out in a unfastened formation, with their elephants primary the charge. The Romans have the numbers, however the Carthaginians have the superior technique. The ground trembles as the 2 forces collide, and the conflict starts offevolved. The air is packed with dust and the screams of fellows. It's not possible to inform who's triumphing.

Hannibal's approach turned into to apply a double-envelopment tactic, once in a while referred to as a "pincer motion." He despatched his brother Hasdrubal to persuade the cavalry on a flank assault, whilst he led the principle pressure in a frontal assault. The Romans were drawn proper into a lure, with their backs to the Aufidus River. Hasdrubal's cavalry lessen off their retreat, whilst Hannibal's forces attacked from the the the front. This aggregate of assaults caused a devastating defeat for the Romans, who suffered heavy casualties.

Hasdrubal's function in the battle became important to Hannibal's technique. First, Hasdrubal needed to lead his cavalry with skills and precision, coordinating his actions with Hannibal's forces. Second, he had to time his assault flawlessly, making sure that he hit the Romans on the proper 2d to seal their future. Third, he needed to instill fear and panic inside the Roman ranks, weakening their morale and making them greater prone to defeat. Finally, Hasdrubal had to have whole undergo in thoughts in his brother's control and judgment, understanding that they had been stopping for a not unusual motive.

This approach is a superb example of the essence of friendship. In order for it to gain success, there needed to be whole consider and loyalty amongst Hannibal, Maharbal, and Hasdrubal. They needed to be completely devoted to their shared aim, and they needed to art work collectively as a team to advantage it. This is an excellent example of how friendship calls for a deep feel of trust, recognize, and common reason. Without these devices, it is no longer viable to gain exceptional matters. So, the Battle of Cannae can be seen as a lesson within the significance of friendship and teamwork.

One of the maximum telling instances of their bond happened after Hannibal's awesome victory. However, but this victory, Hannibal's disability to capitalize on the momentum by using right away marching on Rome has been debated thru historians.

It became on this moment of strategic preference-making that Maharbal's loyalty and friendship shone brightly. Historically stated, Maharbal is stated to have exclaimed to Hannibal, "You understand the manner to win a victory, Hannibal, but you do now not recognize a manner to use it." His phrases, whether or not or no longer an expression of frustration or actual subject for his pal's success, underline the intimate connection amongst Hannibal and Maharbal.

Maharbal's candid assertion pondered the intensity in their friendship. It wasn't definitely a professional alliance cast on the battlefield; it prolonged to some extent wherein Maharbal felt cushty tough Hannibal's selections for the sake in their shared objectives. In this, Maharbal showed the tendencies of a real friend – one that speaks truely, allows, and is unafraid to voice troubles, even to the terrific Hannibal.

The Impact of Meaningful Connections

Meaningful connections keep the energy to profoundly effect our well-being, boom, and huge happiness. These connections move past mere interactions; they're the essence of shared opinions, mutual records, and actual care. The effect of first-rate connections is multi-faceted and resonates at some stage in numerous additives of our lives:

1. Emotional Support:

Meaningful connections function pillars of emotional assist for the duration of hard times. Friends and cherished ones provide a secure vicinity for expression, empathy, and statistics, supplying consolation in moments of vulnerability.

2. Personal Growth:

Interacting with diverse people exposes us to new views, mind, and demanding situations. Meaningful connections turn out to be catalysts for private boom, pushing us to broaden our horizons, encompass trade, and try for self-improvement.

three. Mental Well-being:

Strong social connections are connected to better intellectual health. Meaningful relationships provide a experience of belonging, lessen feelings of loneliness, and make a contribution to common emotional nicely-being.

4. Resilience in Adversity:

During tough times, the help of huge connections may be a deliver of resilience. Whether handling non-public setbacks or societal stressful situations, know-how that there are folks that absolutely care fosters a experience of strength and backbone.

5. Shared Joy and Celebration:

Meaningful connections decorate moments of satisfaction and birthday party. Whether it's far achievements, milestones, or really shared laughter, the presence of others magnifies the exceptional opinions in our lives.

6. Enhanced Empathy and Understanding:

Engaging in massive connections fosters empathy and information. Learning from others' studies and views cultivates a sense of compassion, breaking down boundaries and selling concord.

7. Professional Success:

In the professional realm, significant connections are instrumental. Networking, mentorship, and collaborative partnerships make contributions to career development, skills improvement, and a experience of professional network.

8. Physical Health:

Studies endorse that robust social connections can actually effect bodily fitness. From promoting healthier lifestyles to supplying a aid machine within the direction of ailments, enormous connections play a feature in regular well-being.

nine. Longevity and Quality of Life:

Research indicates that people with robust social ties have a tendency to stay longer and enjoy a better extraordinary of lifestyles. The emotional and sensible useful aid from significant connections contributes to regular health and durability.

10. Sense of Purpose:

Meaningful connections often offer a revel in of motive and belonging. Whether thru familial bonds, friendships, or network affiliations, feeling associated with others gives life a deeper which means that.

In essence, the effect of first rate connections extends a long way beyond the surface of each day interactions. It shapes our identity, affects our alternatives, and office paintings the foundation for a fulfilling and enriched lifestyles. As we navigate the complex net of relationships, the profound have an impact on of those connections will become a testament to the inherent human need for actual and significant bonds.

The Different Shades of Friendship

Friendship, like a kaleidoscope, well-known a rich array of shades and solar sun shades, every contributing to the complex sample of human connection. As we navigate the complicated panorama of relationships, the first rate solar sunglasses of friendship emerge, imparting a diverse spectrum of stories and emotions:

1. Loyal Crimson:

At the middle of profound friendships lies loyalty, a deep pink shade that withstands the exams of time and adversity. Loyal pals stand through your facet, imparting unwavering assist and take delivery of as real with, growing a bond that endures the rigors of lifestyles.

2. Playful Turquoise:

Playful friendships exude the carefree and colourful electricity of turquoise. These friends infuse satisfaction into your existence, growing moments of laughter, shared adventures, and a lightness of being that makes the adventure collectively quality.

Chapter 2: The Foundation Of Friendships

Many philosophers at some stage in information have emphasized the significance of self-reflected picture as a way of records oneself, reaching non-public increase, and leading a huge life.

1. Socrates:

Socrates, a classical Greek fact seeker, is thought for his famous dictum, "Know thyself." He believed that self-knowledge turn out to be the inspiration of attention. Socrates asserted that people who've interplay in self-examination and reflect on their ideals, values, and actions might lead extra virtuous and extraordinary lives.

2. Marcus Aurelius:

As a Stoic fact seeker and Roman Emperor, Marcus Aurelius wrote significantly on self-contemplated photo in his "Meditations." He emphasised the importance of introspection and analyzing one's thoughts and behaviors. Aurelius believed that thru self-popularity and mirrored image, humans ought to benefit tranquility and align their lives with cause and particular feature.

3. Confucius:

Confucius, the Chinese logician, harassed the importance of self-reflected picture in cultivating ethical person. He emphasized the significance of non-prevent self-improvement thru introspection and gaining knowledge of from one's memories. Confucius believed that a virtuous life begins with understanding oneself and striving for private betterment.

4. Immanuel Kant:

Immanuel Kant, a German Enlightenment logician, highlighted self-mirrored image as a key detail of ethical autonomy. He argued that human beings need to appreciably take a look at their moral necessities and act in step with principles that might be universally finished. Kant's ethical philosophy underscores the want for people to reflect on the ethical implications of their actions.

five. Jean-Jacques Rousseau:

Rousseau, a French Enlightenment reality seeker, explored the priority be counted of self-reflected picture in his art work "Confessions." He supplied a candid and introspective account of his very own existence, acknowledging each his virtues and flaws. Rousseau's emphasis on honesty in self-exam brought approximately later thinkers and contributed to the style of autobiographical writing.

6. John Locke:

John Locke, an influential Enlightenment philosopher, believed that self-reflected image became critical for the improvement of private identification. In his "Essay Concerning Human Understanding," Locke proposed that individuals collect statistics via reflected image on their non-public research and interest, shaping their understanding of themselves.

7. Friedrich Nietzsche:

Nietzsche, a German logician, explored the idea of self-meditated photo as regards to the improvement of individuality and the "will to strength." He encouraged people to mirror on their values, query societal norms, and create their personal that means in a international that regularly imposes conformity.

8. Martin Heidegger:

Heidegger, a 20th-century existentialist philosopher, delved into the concept of "authenticity" and the significance of self-meditated picture in uncovering one's real self. He argued that humans need to confront their very private lifestyles and take duty for their selections via introspection.

These philosophers collectively emphasize the transformative potential of self-pondered photograph, viewing it as a path to self-data, ethical development, and a extra right and significant existence.

Identifying Your Values and Interests

Elon Musk's journey began with the co-founding of Zip2, a software program business enterprise, and later X.Com, a web fee organization that in the long run became PayPal. With the achievement of these ventures, Musk won massive wealth, but his pursuits extended a ways beyond monetary fulfillment. Fueled with the aid of his values and pursuits, Musk set his factors of interest on industries with the capability to transform the destiny.

In 2003, Musk primarily based completely Tesla Motors, driven via a profound subject for the environment and a choice to boost up the world's transition to sustainable electricity. At a time whilst electric powered powered vehicles were frequently perceived as impractical, Musk's vision have become to create excessive-performance electric powered powered vehicles that would rival conventional gasoline-powered automobiles. This business enterprise required a huge investment of his very own money and an unwavering dedication to his values. Despite severa disturbing conditions, collectively with skepticism from the auto commercial enterprise employer, Musk endured, and Tesla has due to the truth end up a chief player within the automobile market, revolutionizing the perception of electrical automobiles.

Parallel to his work with Tesla, Musk's interest in area exploration and the concept of making humanity a multi-planetary species added about the creation of SpaceX in 2002. This assignment aimed to reduce space transportation costs and permit the colonization of Mars. Musk's fascination with area dated again to his childhood, and SpaceX have end up the embodiment of his kids desires. The business enterprise finished severa milestones, together with being the first privately-funded agency to release, orbit, and get better a spacecraft. The improvement of the Falcon and Starship rockets showcased Musk's dedication to pushing the bounds of area exploration.

Elon Musk's tale is a tale of tenacity, hazard-taking, and the a achievement alignment of values and interests. His endeavors with Tesla and SpaceX not most effective converted industries however furthermore examined how a deep know-how of private values and the pursuit of actual pastimes can lead to groundbreaking upgrades with international implications. Musk's impact extends past agency; it is a testament to the transformative electricity of aligning one's values and hobbies with a larger imaginative and prescient for the destiny.

Identifying your values and hobbies is a crucial step on the direction to creating friends that don't forget – connections that align in conjunction with your right self and make contributions to significant relationships. Understanding your values includes spotting the thoughts and beliefs which can be essential to your feel of self. Likewise, acknowledging your pastimes unveils the sports and passions that supply you satisfaction and success. In the context of cultivating large friendships, this self-popularity becomes a guiding compass:

1. Authentic Connections:

Identifying your values allows you to are seeking out pals who percentage comparable requirements. When your values align, the muse of the friendship is rooted in authenticity, fostering a deeper connection that withstands the test of time.

2. Shared Passions:

Recognizing your interests lets in you to connect with individuals who percent your passions. Whether it's a love for literature, sports activities, or art work, common hobbies provide a fertile floor for building connections and appealing in sports sports that supply mutual delight.

3. Meaningful Conversations:

Knowing your values helps you've got interplay in conversations that depend. Meaningful friendships thrive on open and sincere verbal exchange, and facts your very non-public values lets in you to particular yourself authentically at the same time as appreciating the views of others.

4. Alignment of Goals:

Identifying shared values and pursuits with buddies often manner aligning your goals. Whether it's miles personal growth, profession aspirations, or manner of lifestyles choices, having pals who apprehend and help your adventure contributes to a supportive and enriching social circle.

5. Respectful Boundaries:

Knowing your values permits you to set and speak barriers successfully. Meaningful friendships are constructed on mutual apprehend, and facts your values lets in you articulate your goals even as respecting the limits of others.

6. Building a Community:

Recognizing shared hobbies permits you to take part in agencies and social circles that resonate along side your passions. This, in turn, enables the natural growth of friendships as you connect with like-minded people in areas in which your values are celebrated.

7. Navigating Differences:

Understanding your values prepares you for navigating variations in a extraordinary way. Meaningful friendships broadly diagnosed and understand variety, and self-recognition permits you to method differing perspectives with empathy and an open mind.

8. Support System:

Friends who percentage your values regularly grow to be a reliable help device. Whether going thru annoying situations or celebrating achievements, the ones connections offer facts, encouragement, and a experience of belonging, fostering a deeper and more enduring bond.

In essence, the adventure to creating friends that depend starts offevolved offevolved with a profound expertise of oneself. By figuring out your values and hobbies, you create a blueprint for actual connections that contribute to a satisfying and sensible social life. As you navigate the landscape of relationships armed with self-cognizance, you are better geared up to attract and nurture friendships that move beyond floor-stage interactions, remodeling the normal into awesome bonds that stand the test of time.

How to Identify Your Values and Interests

Identifying your values and pursuits is a treasured manner that consists of self-reflection and introspection. Here's a step-with the useful resource of-step guide that will help you find out and make clean your values and hobbies:

1. Reflect on Core Beliefs:

Take time to reflect for your middle beliefs and ideas. Consider what matters maximum to you in life, every for my part and on your interactions with others. What ideas manual your selection-making?

2. Examine Past Experiences:

Analyze your past opinions and end up aware about moments at the identical time as you felt fulfilled, proud, or content material. These instances regularly provide clues approximately the values that resonate with you. Conversely, reflect on times even as you felt conflicted or uneasy to apprehend which values were doubtlessly compromised.

three. Prioritize Values:

Once you've got recognized a list of capability values, prioritize them based totally on significance. Consider which values are non-negotiable and which might be greater bendy. This step lets in you apprehend the hierarchy of your values.

4. Explore External Influences:

Consider the affect of outdoor elements which include own family, culture, or society for your values. Evaluate whether or now not positive values are intrinsic to your actual self or if they may be inspired via outside expectancies.

five. Articulate Your Values:

Clearly articulate your values in a written form. Create a list or a assertion that succinctly represents the necessities that rely variety most to you. This can function a reference component for destiny desire-making.

Identifying Your Interests:

1. Reflect on Passions:

Reflect on sports activities or topics that clearly excite and energize you. Consider what you may spend hours doing with out feeling tired. These passions regularly advise your real interests.

2. Explore Curiosities:

Identify regions of interest or subjects which you find exciting. This have to encompass pursuits, fields of check, or sports activities you have got constantly favored to attempt. Exploring those curiosities can bring about the invention of recent hobbies.

3. Assess Current Hobbies:

Evaluate your present day pursuits and pastimes. What sports sports do you definitely gravitate in the route of for your loose time? These modern-day pursuits offer precious insights into what brings you joy.

four. Consider Career Aspirations:

Assess your profession aspirations and hobbies related to your professional life. Are there specific abilties or fields you would like to increase in addition? Connecting your personal pursuits collectively collectively along with your professional dreams can purpose a greater satisfying profession.

5. Experiment and Experience:

Actively engage in new recollections. Attend activities, workshops, or try out unique sports activities to reveal yourself to a whole lot of capability pursuits. Pay hobby on your feelings and reactions in the course of those research.

6. Connect with Like-Minded Individuals:

Connect with folks who percentage comparable pastimes. Engaging in discussions and sports with like-minded humans can deepen your statistics of your very very own passions and introduce you to new ones.

7. Keep a Journal:

Maintain a journal in which you file your thoughts, emotions, and tales related to your values and pursuits. Periodically assessment your mag to come to be aware of patterns and advantage similarly clarity.

8. Seek Feedback:

Talk to friends, circle of relatives, or mentors about your values and interests. Sometimes, outdoor perspectives can provide treasured insights and verify or project your self-discoveries.

Remember that self-discovery is an ongoing way, and it is okay in your values and pursuits to conform over time. Stay open to new reviews and be affected character with yourself as you navigate this adventure of self-exploration.

Embracing Authenticity in Friendships

Embracing authenticity in friendships is a transformative journey that includes cultivating genuine connections, being proper to oneself, and fostering relationships constructed on receive as proper with and openness. Authentic friendships thrive on mutual recognition, information, and the freedom to express one's right self. Here are steps to encompass authenticity for your friendships:

1. Know Yourself:

Authenticity starts offevolved with self-recognition. Take the time to recognize your values, ideals, and aspirations. Knowing who you are permits you to deliver your actual self into your friendships.

2. Be Vulnerable:

Authenticity requires vulnerability. Share your mind, emotions, and memories on the facet of your pals, allowing them to see your real self. Vulnerability fosters a deeper connection and encourages reciprocity. Note that you ought to be careful with who you explicit your vulnerabilities, for a few humans will use the ones in competition to you. They are not your buddies, and you have to be cautious for whoever uses your insecurities in opposition to you.

Chapter 3: Initiating Meaningful Conversations

Overcoming Social Anxiety

Social anxiety, also referred to as social phobia, is a mental circumstance characterised with the aid of an excessive worry of social conditions and the accompanying worry about being negatively judged or evaluated with the aid of others. Individuals with social anxiety regularly experience overwhelming self-awareness and a continual worry of embarrassment or humiliation in social settings.

Key Features of Social Anxiety:

1. Excessive Fear of Negative Evaluation:

Individuals with social anxiety harbor an irrational fear of being judged, criticized, or rejected by manner of others. The worry regularly goes past normal nervousness in social conditions.

2. Avoidance Behavior:

Socially demanding people may fit to fantastic lengths to keep away from situations that trigger their tension. This avoidance can reason not noted possibilities for social interplay and the improvement of significant connections.

3. Physical Symptoms:

Social anxiety can seem bodily, important to symptoms on the side of trembling, sweating, blushing, nausea, or a racing coronary heart. These physical manifestations can further accentuate the concern of being scrutinized.

four. Negative Self-Image:

Individuals with social anxiety often harbor a negative self-photo. They can also moreover apprehend themselves as socially insufficient or fear that others will phrase their perceived flaws, contributing to a cycle of self-doubt.

5. Limited Social Life:

Social tension can bring about a restrained social life, as humans can also moreover avoid gatherings, parties, or maybe one-on-one interactions. This avoidance hinders the improvement of friendships and considerable connections.

6. Impact on Daily Functioning:

Social anxiety can make bigger beyond particular social activities, affecting everyday sports. For instance, creating a phone name, talking up in a meeting, or possibly ordering meals in a restaurant can purpose tension for human beings with social anxiety.

How Social Anxiety Hinders Friendships:

1. Difficulty Initiating Conversations:

Socially disturbing people can also locate it challenging to initiate conversations, fearing capability rejection or judgment. This problem in beginning interactions can avert the natural improvement of friendships.

2. Fear of Rejection:

The fear of rejection is a pervasive component of social anxiety. This fear can prevent human beings from putting themselves in situations wherein they may meet capability buddies or from expressing their actual selves for worry of not being tremendous.

three. Overthinking Social Interactions:

Individuals with social anxiety regularly engage in immoderate rumination approximately beyond and destiny social interactions. This overthinking can bring about heightened self-cognizance and make it hard to be in reality present within the 2nd.

four. Limited Social Skills Development:

Social anxiety can avert the development of social abilities, as people can also keep away from conditions that provide opportunities for workout and improvement. This, in flip, can ward off the potential to navigate and maintain significant friendships.

five. Impact on Self-Esteem:

Persistent social tension can make a contribution to a terrible impact on conceitedness. The normal fear of judgment and perceived social inadequacy can erode self-self perception, making it difficult to just accept as real with one is well worth of forming huge connections.

Overcoming Social Anxiety for Meaningful Friendships:

1. Seek Professional Support:

Therapeutic interventions, inclusive of cognitive-behavioral treatment (CBT) or publicity treatment, may be powerful in addressing social tension. A intellectual fitness expert can provide steerage and strategies for overcoming demanding mind and behaviors.

2. Gradual Exposure:

Gradual exposure to social conditions can desensitize human beings to their fears. Starting with small, practicable steps and frequently difficult tension-scary situations can construct self belief through the years.

three. Challenge Negative Thoughts:

Cognitive restructuring involves hard and converting terrible idea styles. By identifying and hard irrational mind, human beings can adjust their views and reduce anxiety.

4. Social Skills Training:

Learning and working towards social capabilities can enhance self belief in social situations. This can incorporate feature-gambling, conversation education, and acquiring realistic tools for navigating social interactions.

5. Mindfulness and Relaxation Techniques:

Mindfulness and rest techniques, collectively with deep respiratory or meditation, can help control anxiety signs. These practices promote a relaxed and targeted nation of thoughts in social conditions.

6. Join Supportive Groups:

Engaging in sports activities or companies where there's a shared hobby can offer a greater cushty setting for social interaction. Shared pastimes create herbal communique starters and a enjoy of belonging.

7. Set Realistic Goals:

Setting practical and possible social goals can help humans little by little construct self belief. Celebrating small victories reinforces high-quality memories and diminishes the fear related to social interactions.

eight. Practice Self-Compassion:

Developing self-compassion involves treating oneself with kindness and information. Recognizing that everyone makes errors and recollections social demanding situations can alleviate self-imposed strain.

Overcoming social anxiety is a slow way that consists of self-reputation, expert assist, and persistent try. As human beings artwork in the route of handling their anxiety, they open the door to forming significant connections and friendships that make a contribution to a richer and additional enjoyable social existence.

Strategies for Approaching New People

Oscar Wilde, the Irish poet and playwright, have become a considerable discern in London's social scene throughout the late 19th century. His wit and appeal made him a sought-after traveller at dinner events and gatherings. His conversations had been identified for their cleverness, humor, and the ability to satirize the societal norms of the time.

Winston Churchill changed into virtually a masterful conversationalist, and lots of anecdotes and fees showcase his wit, humor, and functionality to connect to humans. One famous instance occurred in the course of a event with Lady Astor, a fellow Member of Parliament and the primary female MP to take her seat. The had been recognized for his or her active exchanges, sometimes bordering on sharp banter.Churchill have grow to be diagnosed for his sharp and frequently humorous feedback, showcasing his mastery of language and functionality to have interaction in good sized conversations. A few extremely good examples:

1. Exchange with Lady Astor:

Lady Astor: "Winston, if you have been my husband, I'd poison your tea."

Churchill: "Nancy, if I have been your husband, I'd drink it."

2. Parliamentary Wit:

On one event, after an opponent accused him of being under the influence of alcohol:

Churchill: "Yes, I am below the have an effect on of alcohol. But you're mad, and I will be sober in the morning."

3. Exchange with Bessie Braddock:

Bessie Braddock: "Sir, you're inebriated."

Churchill: "And you, madam, are unpleasant. But in the morning, I will be sober, and you may although be unpleasant."

four. Letter to Churchill's Wife, Clementine:

In a letter to his spouse in a few unspecified time within the destiny of a especially difficult political 2d:

Churchill: "My Darling Clemmie, inside the event of an invasion through the Nazis, I shall declare myself Leader of the Opposition."

These instances replicate Churchill's wit, smart comebacks, and capability to use humor to diffuse anxiety. While those fees might not seize precise historical conversations, they provide a glimpse into Churchill's conversational fashion, illustrating his knack for memorable and impactful conversation.

The Art of Small Talk and Meaningful Conversations

Introducing ice-breaking techniques right right into a conversation is an artwork that could rework preliminary awkwardness into a snug and attractive interaction. Whether in a social putting, a professional environment, or assembly someone for the primary time, breaking the ice is ready setting up a connection and growing an environment that encourages open communication. Some powerful ice-breaking techniques you can try out encompass:

1. Start with a Genuine Compliment:

Begin the conversation via imparting a honest reward. It may be approximately some component the individual is carrying, a current fulfillment, or a pleasing trait you have got got positioned. A right praise can without delay create a high-quality surroundings.

Chapter 4: Building Lasting Connections

On a cold day in January 1942, a person named Leon Greenman and his accomplice, Else, have been taken from their domestic in Amsterdam and transported to a Nazi consciousness camp known as Auschwitz. They had no idea what awaited them there, however they knew that they might be separated and may face implausible trouble. When they arrived on the camp, they were separated into particular sections primarily based totally on their gender. Leon in no way found his wife over again. He emerge as placed to art work in a labor camp, in which he worked extended hours and have become given little or no meals. He have grow to be constantly bloodless and hungry, and he needed to learn how to live on in a brutal environment.

After severa months, Leon met every distinct prisoner named Hugo Gryn. Hugo became a Czechoslovakian Jew who've been a rabbi earlier than the conflict. The men at once struck up a friendship, bonding over their shared faith and lifestyle. They spent hours speaking about their lives before the struggle, their families, and their hopes for the destiny. They shared what little meals that they had and did what they may to help every considered one of a kind live on. Even despite the fact that they had been dwelling in a place of terror and dying, they decided consolation and companionship in every other's organisation.

For the next three years, Leon and Hugo did their great to keep every other going. They shared recollections of their lives earlier than the conflict, advised jokes to make every wonderful giggle, and stored every exclusive's spirits up. Even in the darkest of times, they discovered ways to discover this means that and motive of their lives. In the spring of 1945, the Russian military liberated Auschwitz, and Leon and Hugo have been loose. They hugged every different tightly, overcome with pleasure and luxury. They had survived toward all odds, and they had every unique to thank for it.

After the battle, Leon and Hugo went their separate strategies. Leon decrease back to England, in which he worked to raise interest approximately the horrors of the Holocaust. Hugo eventually have end up a rabbi in England, in which he taught and inspired others alongside collectively along with his faith and compassion. Despite living in precise worldwide locations, Leon and Hugo remained near buddies for the relaxation of their lives. They wrote letters to each unique, sharing records and memories in their time together at Auschwitz. Even although that they'd skilled not possible suffering, they never lost wish or their capability to locate because of this in life.

In the overdue Nineties, Leon and Hugo had the opportunity to peer every one-of-a-kind one final time. They have been each of their 90s, and their fitness modified into failing. They met in a inn in London and spent hours reminiscing approximately their lives and their friendship. They talked about the love and guide that they'd given every terrific for the duration of their darkest moments. And, in the end, they stated their goodbyes, understanding that their friendship have been a deliver of energy and comfort for each of them. In the stop, they were thankful for the bond they had shared, a bond that had been solid inside the fires of Auschwitz.

The Qualities of Meaningful Friendships

While now not anybody will experience the horrors of a interest camp, we're able to but have a study from the tale of Leon and Hugo. The key to their friendship became no longer the conditions they faced, however the processes wherein they supported every other. In our non-public lives, we can assemble lasting connections with the resource of being there for every exclusive via the coolest instances and the awful. We can provide a listening ear, a shoulder to cry on, or a helping hand. Even the smallest gestures can make a massive difference in a person's existence. By being there for every one in all a type, we're capable of create bonds that closing a life-time.

Meaningful friendships are characterized with the useful resource of a very particular mixture of abilities that pass beyond floor-degree interactions. These capabilities contribute to the depth, acquire as right with, and mutual assist that outline lasting and great connections. Here are a few key traits of significant friendships:

1. Trust and Reliability:

Trustworthiness: Meaningful friendships are built on a foundation of consider. Friends rely on each special to be honest, dependable, and genuine to their word.

Reliability: Being there for each other in every real times and terrible fosters a sense of reliability. Consistency and dependability aid the bond among buddies.

2. Authenticity and Open Communication:

Authenticity: True friends can be themselves without worry of judgment. Authenticity creates a stable place wherein people experience common for who they're.

Open Communication: Meaningful friendships thrive on open and sincere communique. The functionality to specific thoughts, feelings, and troubles contributes to a deeper expertise.

three. Mutual Respect:

Respect: Respect for every other's reviews, barriers, and individuality is important. Meaningful friendships honor differences and promote a experience of mutual understanding.

four. Shared Values and Interests:

Common Ground: Having shared values and hobbies gives a strong basis for connection. Shared studies and passions make a contribution to a enjoy of camaraderie.

five. Empathy and Compassion:

Empathy: Understanding and sharing in every exceptional's emotions creates a compassionate connection. Empathy strengthens the emotional bond among pals.

Compassion: Offering assist and kindness in the end of difficult instances demonstrates compassion. Meaningful friendships comprise a actual situation for every one-of-a-kind's nicely-being.

6. Positive Influence:

Encouragement: Meaningful pals encourage and uplift every one-of-a-type. They characteristic property of encouragement, motivating personal growth and self-development.

Positive Influence: Being a brilliant impact includes fostering an environment that nurtures each unique's strengths and aspirations.

7. Reciprocity and Equality:

Reciprocity: Meaningful friendships incorporate a supply-and-take dynamic. Both friends contribute to the connection, ensuring stability and reciprocity.

Equality: Friends see every unique as equals, respecting each extraordinary's contributions, reviews, and dreams inside the friendship.

8. Adaptability and Acceptance:

Adaptability: Friendships evolve through the years, and massive connections adapt to existence's modifications. Flexibility and flexibility make contributions to the sturdiness of the relationship.

Acceptance: Embracing each one of a kind's flaws and imperfections fosters elegance. Meaningful buddies apprehend each special for who they're, with out the need for perfection.

9. Shared History and Loyalty:

Shared History: Building a massive friendship frequently includes developing a shared history. Shared critiques create a bond that withstands the take a look at of time.

Loyalty: Meaningful friendships are characterised thru loyalty. Friends stand via manner of every one-of-a-kind thru traumatic conditions and triumphs, demonstrating unwavering resource.

10. Joy in Each Other's Success:

Celebration: True friends find out pleasure in each other's successes. Celebrating achievements and milestones together strengthens the feel of shared happiness.

eleven. Forgiveness and Resolution:

Forgiveness: Mistakes are inevitable, but forgiveness allows friendships to heal. The ability to forgive and are in search of choice contributes to the resilience of the connection.

12. Unconditional Love:

Unconditional Support: Meaningful friendships contain unconditional love and assist. Friends offer a feel of protection, data they'll be valued for actually being themselves.

In essence, significant friendships are dynamic, evolving connections that decorate our lives. These traits form the cloth of deep, enduring relationships that deliver achievement, pleasure, and a experience of belonging.

Fostering Trust and Loyalty

Building and fostering receive as actual with and loyalty is essential for cultivating robust, meaningful relationships, whether they are friendships, partnerships, or professional connections. Trust and loyalty form the inspiration of lasting bonds and make a contribution to the general nicely-being of humans and the health of the connection. Here are a few strategies to foster take transport of as actual with and loyalty:

1. Open and Honest Communication:

Transparency: Be open and sincere for your conversation. Transparency builds agree with with the aid of the usage of growing an surroundings in which facts is shared brazenly, and there are not any hidden agendas.

Active Listening: Demonstrate lively listening capabilities to show that you value and understand the alternative individual's mind-set. Understanding every different contributes to a stronger bond.

2. Consistency and Reliability:

Keep Commitments: Consistently retaining commitments and following via on guarantees establishes reliability. Reliability is a key factor of do not forget, as it suggests that you may bear in mind on.

Consistent Behavior: Demonstrate regular conduct over time. Predictability fosters a feel of protection, contributing to the improvement of believe.

three. Empathy and Understanding:

Empathetic Listening: Show empathy by means of actively taking note of the feelings and issues of others. Understanding each different's emotions creates a deeper connection.

Put Yourself in Their Shoes: Try to apprehend the alternative man or woman's attitude and memories. Seeing subjects from their element of view promotes empathy and strengthens the connection.

four. Accountability and Ownership:

Take Responsibility: When mistakes happen, take possession and duty. Acknowledge errors, test from them, and artwork in the course of making amends. Accountability builds consider by using manner of way of demonstrating integrity.

Problem-Solving Together: Collaborate on solutions even as challenges stand up. Facing problems as a crew strengthens the bond and reinforces loyalty.

five. Respect for Boundaries:

Acknowledge Boundaries: Respect the bounds set via manner of the opportunity man or woman. Understanding and acknowledging private obstacles contribute to a experience of safety within the relationship.

Clearly Communicate Boundaries: Clearly speak your private boundaries to make sure mutual know-how and appreciate.

6. Relational Consistency:

Consistent Support: Be constantly supportive at some point of each accurate and difficult times. Reliable assist contributes to a experience of loyalty and deepens the emotional connection.

Celebrate Successes Together: Celebrate achievements and milestones together. Sharing in every one-of-a-kind's successes reinforces the remarkable factors of the relationship.

7. Demonstrate Trustworthiness:

Act with Integrity: Uphold a excessive famous of integrity in your moves and selections. Consistently acting with integrity builds take shipping of as proper with and reinforces your trustworthiness.

Avoid Gossip: Refrain from gossip or behaviors that might undermine do not forget. Trust is effortlessly eroded at the same time as humans experience their terms or movements can be used towards them.

8. Invest Time and Effort:

Quality Time: Invest great time inside the courting. Spending time together fosters a deeper connection and demonstrates dedication.

Make an Effort: Show that you are inclined to invest strive into the connection. Acts of kindness and thoughtfulness deliver a boost to the emotional bond.

9. Celebrate Individuality:

Respect Differences: Embrace and feature an top notch time the distinctiveness of the opportunity individual. Respecting and valuing variations make a contribution to a experience of loyalty as every people experience traditional for who they're.

10. Express Gratitude:

Gratitude: Regularly particular gratitude for the presence and contributions of the alternative individual. Feeling favored enhances feelings of loyalty and strengthens the connection.

Fostering maintain in mind and loyalty is an ongoing technique that requires determination, verbal exchange, and mutual try. By prioritizing the ones characteristics on your relationships, you create a sturdy foundation for massive and enduring connections.

Navigating the Depths of Mutual Support

Mutual assistance is a cornerstone of meaningful relationships, imparting a supply of power and resilience within the face of life's traumatic situations. Navigating the depths of mutual assist consists of growing a reciprocal and uplifting dynamic that enriches the connection amongst human beings. Here are techniques for fostering mutual resource:

1. Active Listening and Validation:

Attentive Listening: Practice active being attentive to certainly apprehend the alternative character's mind and emotions. Being present and engaged demonstrates actual care and guide.

Validate Emotions: Validate the opposite man or woman's feelings by using the use of the use of acknowledging their emotions with out judgment. Offering validation fosters a revel in of records and aid.

2. Empathy and Compassion:

Put Yourself in Their Shoes: Cultivate empathy with the resource of using trying to apprehend the opposite character's attitude. Empathy builds a deeper connection and enhances the incredible of mutual useful resource.

Compassionate Responses: Respond to demanding conditions with compassion. Offering phrases of comfort and encouragement strengthens the bond and creates a supportive environment.

3. Celebrate Successes Together:

Shared Joy: Celebrate every particular's successes and achievements. Sharing in moments of delight reinforces the high best elements of the connection and contributes to a supportive environment.

Acknowledge Efforts: Acknowledge and understand the efforts made with the resource of the alternative man or woman. Recognizing their accomplishments, regardless of how small, reinforces a supportive thoughts-set.

4. Be Reliable and Consistent:

Dependability: Be dependable and regular in offering useful resource. Consistency builds trust, and dependability is important for growing a stable vicinity in the courting.

Follow Through on Commitments: If you make a decision to supplying manual or assist, have a examine via on your commitments. Reliability enhances the texture of mutual assist.

5. Encourage Personal Growth:

Supportive Encouragement: Encourage personal increase and self-improvement. Offer terms of encouragement and offer manual for endeavors that make contributions to the alternative person's development.

Chapter 5: Resilience In Friendships

Friendships, whilst immensely worthwhile, also can face diverse annoying situations that require know-how, verbal exchange, and mutual try to triumph over. Recognizing and addressing those commonplace challenges is important for retaining healthy and lasting relationships. Here are some not unusual disturbing conditions in friendships:

1. Communication Breakdown:

Misunderstandings: Lack of clean communication can result in misunderstandings. Differences in conversation styles or failure to unique thoughts and feelings openly can also additionally make a contribution to misinterpretations.

2. Changing Priorities and Life Transitions:

Shifts in Priorities: Individuals may additionally go through changes in priorities due to profession upgrades, circle of relatives duties, or non-public growth. These shifts can effect the quantity of time and power to be had for the friendship.

Life Transitions: Major life sports which include transferring, starting a own family, or pursuing better training can create bodily or emotional distance between buddies.

three. Jealousy and Envy:

Comparisons: Comparisons and emotions of jealousy can stand up, mainly if one pal perceives the opposite as reaching more fulfillment or experiencing more happiness. Navigating the ones emotions calls for open communique and reassurance.

4. Differing Expectations:

Unmet Expectations: Friends might also have extremely good expectancies concerning the nature and degree of the friendship. Unspoken or unmet expectations can result in sadness and frustration.

5. Conflict and Disagreements:

Differing Perspectives: Disagreements and conflicts can emerge from differing perspectives, values, or evaluations. Handling conflicts maturely and finding not unusual ground is vital for resolving troubles.

6. Lack of Reciprocity:

One-Sided Effort: In some instances, one buddy also can revel in that they may be investing more time, attempt, or emotional power into the friendship than the other. Achieving stability and reciprocity is essential for the longevity of the relationship.

7. Unresolved Issues:

Avoidance: Avoiding or failing to address underlying problems can bring about unresolved anxiety. Over time, unaddressed issues may additionally moreover expand and negatively impact the friendship.

8. Competitiveness:

Unhealthy Competition: A enjoy of competitiveness, whether in private achievements or relationships, can stress friendships. Fostering a supportive environment and celebrating every one-of-a-type's successes can mitigate this mission.

nine. External Influences:

Influence of Others: External elements, which includes the have an effect on of diverse social circles, relationships, or societal pressures, could have an impact on the dynamics of a friendship.

10. Personal Growth and Change:

Evolution of Individuals: Personal growth and trade are inevitable, and buddies can also additionally moreover evolve in exquisite recommendations. Navigating those changes on the equal time as final supportive is critical for the friendship's resilience.

eleven. Social Media and Communication Style:

Impact of Social Media: The role of social media in friendships can introduce disturbing conditions, from misinterpretation of on line interactions to emotions of exclusion.

Differences in Communication Styles: Varied communique options, at the side of reliance on digital communication in choice to stand-to-face interactions, may additionally effect the depth of the friendship.

12. Distance and Time Constraints:

Geographical Distance: Physical distance, whether or now not due to relocation or one-of-a-type elements, can create worrying conditions in retaining normal face-to-face interactions.

Busy Schedules: Demanding schedules and time constraints can restrict the availability of pals to connect and spend time collectively.

thirteen. Betrayal of Trust:

Violations of Trust: Instances of betrayal, breaches of confidentiality, or moves that undermine believe can considerably strain or maybe prevent a friendship.

14. Lack of Boundaries:

Invasion of Privacy: A loss of respect for private barriers, along with regular interference or unsolicited recommendation, can stress the friendship.

15. Different Life Stages:

Life Milestones: Friends can also find out themselves in outstanding existence stages, together with starting households or pursuing superior education, important to disparities in existence and priorities.

sixteen. Cultural or Lifestyle Differences:

Diversity in Backgrounds: Differences in cultural backgrounds or existence may contribute to misunderstandings or stressful conditions in referring to every specific.

Addressing the ones demanding situations consists of open communication, empathy, and a dedication to running thru issues. Friends who navigate those hurdles collectively often emerge with stronger, extra resilient relationships.

Communication as a Key to Resolution

Effective conversation is a critical key to resolving conflicts and overcoming challenges in friendships. When friends come across issues or misunderstandings, open and sincere conversation gives a pathway to expertise, empathy, and locating common floor. Here are essential elements of communication as a key to preference in friendships:

1. Active Listening:

Attentiveness: Practice lively listening to sincerely understand your friend's angle. Pay interest, avoid interrupting, and display which you fee their thoughts and feelings.

Reflective Responses: Reflect again what you have got heard to make certain readability and show which you are actively engaged within the communique.

2. Expressing Thoughts and Feelings Clearly:

Use "I" Statements: Express your mind and feelings the use of "I" statements to hold your memories with out assigning blame. For instance, say, "I revel in harm whilst..." in preference to "You continuously..."

3. Avoiding Assumptions:

Seek Clarification: If some element is unsure, ask for rationalization as opposed to making assumptions. Misunderstandings regularly stand up from assumptions that can be effortlessly clarified thru verbal exchange.

4. Choosing the Right Time and Place:

Select Appropriate Moments: Timing is critical in addressing concerns. Choose a time and location conducive to an open and targeted communique, ensuring minimum distractions and interruptions.

five. Maintaining Calm and Respectful Tone:

Stay Calm: Emotional discussions can come to be heated, but it's far essential to stay calm and composed. Take breaks if critical to keep away from escalating tensions.

Respectful Language: Use respectful and non-confrontational language. Avoid harsh or accusatory tones which could initiate defensiveness.

6. Expressing Empathy:

Acknowledge Feelings: Show empathy with the resource of acknowledging your buddy's emotions. Validation fosters knowledge and contributes to a extra fine communicate.

Put Yourself in Their Shoes: Try to recognize the state of affairs out of your pal's mindset. Demonstrating empathy creates a bridge of knowledge.

7. Using "I" Language Instead of "You" Language:

"I" Language Encourages Ownership: Phrasing issues with "I" language encourages personal possession of emotions and research. It promotes a collaborative method to problem-fixing.

eight. Focusing at the Issue, Not the Person:

Separate Behavior from Person: Address the unique problem in desire to creating it approximately your buddy's character. This method prevents protective reactions and continues the communique targeted on locating answers.

9. Seeking Solutions Together:

Collaborative Problem-Solving: Approach conflicts as a set, searching for at the same time agreeable answers. Discuss potential resolutions and be open to compromise.

10. Understanding Different Perspectives:

Value Diversity of Opinions: Recognize that human beings have one-of-a-type perspectives, and those versions make a contribution to the richness of the friendship. Embrace variety in thoughts and evaluations.

eleven. Apologizing and Forgiving:

Sincere Apologies: If you have got got carried out a component in the struggle, provide a sincere apology. Acknowledge errors and specific a strength of will to outstanding change.

Forgiveness: Cultivate forgiveness. Once an problem is resolved, permit bypass of resentment and circulate beforehand with a smooth slate.

12. Establishing Clear Boundaries:

Discuss and Agree on Boundaries: Clearly talk and agree upon barriers to save you future misunderstandings. Establishing mutual expectations fosters a extra healthy friendship.

thirteen. Non-Verbal Communication:

Body Language: Pay hobby to non-verbal cues. Body language can carry feelings and reactions that won't be expressed verbally.

14. Revisiting the Issue if Necessary:

Ongoing Check-Ins: Periodically test in with each other to ensure that resolutions are going for walks and that each occasions are glad. Be open to revisiting the issue if vital.

15. Learning and Growing Together:

Viewing Conflicts as Opportunities: Approach conflicts as possibilities for increase and gaining knowledge of. Friendships that navigate and clear up annoying situations together often emerge more potent and greater resilient.

By incorporating those verbal exchange techniques, buddies can create an surroundings in which conflicts are addressed constructively, main to extra expertise, reinforced bonds, and a more resilient friendship.

Forgiveness and Growth in Relationships

Forgiveness is a powerful strain in relationships, contributing to recuperation, growth, and the strengthening of emotional bonds. It lets in human beings to transport beyond hurtful research and create a basis for splendid transformation. Here are key additives of forgiveness and growth in relationships:

1. Understanding Forgiveness:

Release of Resentment: Forgiveness consists of letting go of resentment, anger, or bad emotions associated with a perceived wrongdoing.

Not Excusing Behavior: Forgiving a person could now not recommend excusing or condoning their movements. It's a personal preference to release the emotional burden in your non-public nicely-being.

2. Benefits of Forgiveness:

Emotional Healing: Forgiveness contributes to emotional recuperation, lowering strain, anxiety, and feelings of hostility.

Restoration of Trust: In the context of relationships, forgiveness can pave the manner for the recuperation of keep in mind and rebuilding of the relationship.

3. Personal Growth:

Learning from Challenges: Forgiveness permits humans to investigate and grow from demanding situations. It fosters resilience and the potential to navigate difficulties with grace.

Self-Reflection: The manner of forgiveness often includes self-mirrored photo, permitting humans to benefit insights into their own emotions, triggers, and private boundaries.

Chapter 6: Expanding Your Social Horizons

In the 14th century, amidst the grandeur of the Islamic Golden Age, a Moroccan scholar and explorer named Ibn Battuta set out on a super adventure. His quest wasn't limited to geographical discovery on my own; it become an excursion into the hearts and minds of diverse cultures, an exploration of the human revel in in all its intricacies.

Ibn Battuta's journey surpassed the bounds of his recognised global, spanning over 75,000 miles at some point of Africa, the Middle East, Asia, and Europe. His travels were no longer simplest a testomony to geographical exploration but a party of the multitude of human memories ready to be opened up.

As he traversed bustling bazaars, serene oases, and the courts of a ways flung kings, Ibn Battuta failed to in reality collect geographical statistics; he solid connections. His tales echo the profound impact of engaging with unique cultures, converting mind, and embracing the splendor of variety. Ibn Battuta's odyssey stands as a beacon, reminding us that our personal horizons are restricted simplest by way of way of the quantity of our hobby and willingness to connect to the arena round us.

The Benefits of Diverse Friendships

Diverse friendships, those usual with human beings from various backgrounds, cultures, and views, supply a large number of benefits that beautify our lives in profound techniques. Embracing range in our social circles opens doors to new opinions, broadens our knowledge of the arena, and fosters non-public growth. Here are a number of the vital element advantages of cultivating numerous friendships:

1. Expanded Perspectives:

Cultural Insights: Friends from various backgrounds provide particular insights into their cultures, traditions, and strategies of existence. Exposure to one-of-a-type perspectives expands our worldview and worrying conditions preconceived notions.

2. Enhanced Creativity and Problem-Solving:

Diverse Perspectives: In diverse friendships, each character brings a unique set of experiences and viewpoints. Collaborating with friends from severa backgrounds enhances creativity and trouble-solving thru tapping right into a broader pool of thoughts.

three. Cultural Exchange and Learning:

Language and Customs: Diverse friendships provide possibilities for cultural trade, allowing us to have a look at new languages, customs, and traditions. This enriching experience deepens our expertise of the sector's variety.

4. Increased Empathy and Compassion:

Understanding Different Experiences: Interacting with pals who've exceptional lifestyles evaluations fosters empathy and compassion. Learning about their stressful conditions and triumphs lets in us to better apprehend the human enjoy in its numerous office work.

5. Personal Growth and Self-Discovery:

Challenging Comfort Zones: Diverse friendships often consist of stepping out of our consolation zones. This way of navigating first-rate perspectives and adapting to new opinions contributes to non-public increase and self-discovery.

6. Breaking Stereotypes:

Humanizing Differences: Building relationships with people from various backgrounds permits damage down stereotypes. By humanizing versions, friendships become a effective device for fostering information and dismantling prejudices.

7. Cultivation of Open-Mindedness:

Acceptance of Differences: Embracing numerous friendships cultivates open-mindedness. It encourages us to realize and accept versions in choice to viewing them as boundaries.

eight. Networking and Professional Opportunities:

Diverse Networks: Diverse friendships enlarge our social networks, growing possibilities for expert increase. Access to some of views may be remarkable in the place of job and in pursuing career opportunities.

9. Resilience in Adversity:

Broad Support System: Diverse friendships contribute to a substantial useful resource device. Having pals from numerous backgrounds offers certainly one of a type belongings of help, strengthening our resilience in times of adversity.

10. Celebration of Diversity:

Shared Celebrations: Diverse friendships create opportunities for shared celebrations. Festivals, vacations, and cultural events grow to be moments of mutual appreciation, fostering a experience of concord amidst variety.

eleven. Social and Emotional Well-Being:

Positive Influence: Diverse friendships were associated with extra suitable social and emotional well-being. The effective have an effect on of supportive friends from high-quality backgrounds can make a contribution to conventional life pride.

12. Global Awareness:

Understanding Global Issues: Friends with diverse backgrounds make a contribution to a higher information of worldwide troubles. Conversations approximately worldwide activities and demanding situations end up more nuanced, knowledgeable, and empathetic.

thirteen. Lifelong Learning:

Continuous Education: Diverse friendships create a continuous studying surroundings.

Friends turn out to be educators, sharing understanding about their backgrounds, pastimes, and knowledge.

14. Fostering Inclusivity:

Promotion of Inclusivity: Being part of numerous friendships promotes inclusivity. By constructing connections that bypass beyond cultural, racial, and societal limitations, we actively contribute to creating a greater inclusive international.

15. Lasting and Meaningful Relationships:

Deep Bonds: Diverse friendships frequently result in lasting and extensive relationships. Shared studies, mutual apprehend, and an appreciation for range useful resource the bonds among buddies.

In essence, numerous friendships now not quality contribute to the mosaic of our social lives but additionally play a pivotal position in shaping a greater interconnected and expertise international community. As we encompass the blessings of various friendships, we now not satisfactory increase our man or woman lives however moreover contribute to the more tapestry of humanity.

Cultivating a Socially Rich Life

Cultivating a socially wealthy life includes intentional efforts to construct and hold massive connections with a severa array of human beings. It is going past mere socializing, emphasizing the first-class and intensity of relationships. Here are techniques for fostering a socially wealthy life:

1. Diversify Your Social Circles:

Explore Varied Interests: Engage in sports activities that align collectively together with your interests but additionally screen you to new human beings. This diversification can motive connections with people from particular backgrounds and perspectives.

2. Attend Social and Community Events:

Local Gatherings: Participate in nearby activities, network gatherings, and social meet-ups. These environments offer possibilities to satisfy new humans and foster connections with those who percent commonplace pastimes.

3. Be Open to New Experiences:

Embrace Novelty: Say certain to new opinions and possibilities. Whether it's trying a new hobby, attending a workshop, or becoming a member of a club, being open-minded expands the opportunities for social connections.

4. Volunteer and Give Back:

Community Engagement: Volunteer for motives you're enthusiastic about. Not most effective does this make contributions to the community, but it additionally introduces you to love-minded folks that share your determination to growing a amazing effect.

five. Cultivate Authenticity:

Be Genuine: Authenticity is the foundation of meaningful connections. Be your self, precise your right mind and feelings, and lure friends who admire you for who you are.

6. Initiate Social Invitations:

Take the Lead: Be proactive in organizing social sports sports. Initiate invitations for espresso, gatherings, or outings. This demonstrates your dedication to nurturing relationships.

7. Stay Connected with Old Friends:

Reconnect: Reach out to vintage pals and pals. Reviving connections from the past can upload depth to your social community and rekindle large relationships.

eight. Invest Time in Existing Relationships:

Quality Time: Prioritize excellent time with contemporary friends. Regular interactions, whether or not in individual or honestly, improve the bonds and hold the electricity of relationships.

Chapter 7: Prioritizing And Investing In Connections

In the colorful heartbeat of New York, inseparable friends, Jonathan and Michael, navigated college desires. As the years unfolded, existence's needs led them along divergent paths. Jonathan thrived in finance, even as Michael embraced the unpredictable rhythm of freelance arts. Late-night time time time conversations yielded to sporadic texts, wants to echoes.

Amidst the city's pulsating electricity, Jonathan and Michael encountered each different at a mutual buddy's wedding ceremony, the gravitational pull of shared recollections breaking through the restrictions of time. The reunion sparked a popularity—a void that had silently grown between them. Jonathan, reflecting on the fulfillment he performed in his profession, felt a hollowness that no organisation accolade have to fill. The camaraderie with Michael, the confidant who had witnessed the adventure's each twist, had end up echo.

Michael, too, sensed the absence of the collaborator whose presence had fueled his contemporary hobbies. The vibrancy in their shared dreams had dimmed in the face of life's relentless pace. As they stood amidst the celebration, the space of their lives have end up palpable, urging them to reevaluate the priorities that had led them to date.

It become a chance come across, but it bore the weight of a aware preference. Jonathan and Michael, spotting the toll their busy lives had taken on their friendship, devoted to bridging the space. They set aside time—a espresso in some unspecified time in the future of a lunch damage, a weekend getaway—prioritizing their connection over the wishes in their careers.

In the quiet corners of a bustling town, conversations have been rekindled, laughter echoed, and the shared dreams of yesteryears positioned a voice another time. The bonds of proper friendship, once overlooked, commenced out to reclaim their significance.

Jonathan decided that the aid of a real pal brought a size to his successes and worrying conditions that no boardroom dialogue may additionally moreover need to provide.

Michael, in turn, determined renewed inspiration in the shared dreams that had long-mounted their university years. The unpredictable rhythm of the freelance arts gained a modern day melody even as harmonized with the unwavering help of a friend who had stood the test of time.

The information in their journey opened up in the intentional prioritization of their friendship. Coffee preserve conversations changed into late-night time time time dinners, and weekend getaways evolved into cherished traditions. The void have become modified with the resource of a tapestry of shared critiques, woven with the threads of laughter, statistics, and shared dreams.

As the seasons changed in the metropolis that in no way sleeps, so did the dynamics of Jonathan and Michael's friendship. What began as a risk come across at a marriage converted right right right into a planned choice to nurture and prioritize a connection that held immeasurable price. Their story have emerge as a testament to the profound effect of friendships at the same time as deliberately cherished, rekindled, and allowed to flourish amidst the stressful landscape of lifestyles.

Investing time and energy in giant connections

Investing time and energy in meaningful connections is a deliberate and transformative choice that holds the capacity to supplement our lives in profound techniques. In a worldwide that often actions at a normal pace, in which digital interactions can outnumber face-to-face conversations, the act of creating an investment in real connections will become a effective and intentional determination.

The Currency of Time:

Time is a precious commodity, and the manner we pick out to spend it reflects our priorities. Investing time in massive connections consists of dedicating moments to shared opinions, whether or not it is a heartfelt verbal exchange over espresso, a leisurely walk within the park, or genuinely being gift inside the company of pals. These moments create a foreign exchange of memories that appreciates over time, forming the inspiration of lasting and loved relationships.

Nurturing Emotional Bonds:

Meaningful connections thrive on emotional bonds. Investing electricity in information the emotions, desires, and aspirations of our buddies deepens the connection. It requires lively listening, empathy, and the willingness to be observed in each satisfied and hard moments. Nurturing emotional bonds fosters a experience of accept as true with and reciprocity, strengthening the material of the relationship.

Shared Experiences as Investments:

Investing in giant connections consists of growing shared reviews. Whether it is embarking on adventures, celebrating milestones, or weathering storms together, the ones shared moments end up the dividends of our investments. The richness of a connection often lies inside the tapestry of recollections woven via joint endeavors and the mutual increase that accompanies them.

Quality Over Quantity:

In the vicinity of connections, quality trumps quantity. It's not about the sheer type of pals however the depth of the relationships. Investing in a few real connections lets in for a more profound facts of every distinct's lives, dreams, and worrying situations. It's a conscious choice to recognition on the relationships that during reality depend.

Weathering the Tests of Time:

Meaningful connections are resilient. They face up to the checks of time, distance, and changing occasions. Investing in the ones connections consists of a determination to weathering the inevitable worrying situations that existence provides. It's the understanding that, like all funding, the returns won't continuously be immediate however are frequently greater massive in the long run.

Reciprocal Investments:

True connections thrive on reciprocity. Investing time and electricity in extensive connections is a -way street in which every events make contributions to the increase and well-being of the relationship. The act of giving and receiving creates a balanced and harmonious dynamic, fostering a experience of mutual useful resource.

Cultivating a Supportive Ecosystem:

Investing in big connections is akin to cultivating a supportive surroundings. Just as a lawn calls for care, interest, and nourishment, so do our relationships. This intentional investment creates an environment in which human beings can flourish, offering every one in all a kind encouragement, knowledge, and a enjoy of belonging.

Enhancing Personal Well-Being:

The returns on making an funding in huge connections growth beyond the relational realm to non-public properly-being. Studies constantly highlight the terrific effect of robust social connections on highbrow and emotional fitness. A community of supportive buddies contributes to a enjoy of cause, belonging, and ordinary life pleasure.

In essence, investing time and energy in full-size connections is a aware preference so one can pay dividends a protracted manner past the preliminary investment. It's a dedication to growing a tapestry of shared evaluations, emotional bonds, and mutual boom. As we navigate the intricacies of our social landscape, allow us to understand the transformative energy of intentional connections, expertise that the richness of existence regularly lies in the depth and authenticity of the relationships we pick to nurture.

The Impact of Meaningful Friendships on Well-Being

The effect of enormous friendships on well-being is profound and a protracted manner-reaching. Research constantly underscores the effective have an impact on that robust social connections have on intellectual, emotional, or even physical health. Here's an exploration of the multifaceted impact of massive friendships on frequent nicely-being:

1. Emotional Support:

Buffering Stress: Meaningful friendships characteristic a buffer towards pressure. The emotional help from buddies allows people cope with existence's annoying situations, reducing the horrible consequences of pressure on intellectual health.

2. Sense of Belonging:

Reducing Isolation: Meaningful friendships offer a revel in of belonging. The feeling of being understood, ordinary, and related reduces emotions of isolation, promoting intellectual properly-being.

3. Improved Mental Health:

Reducing Anxiety and Depression: Strong social connections are associated with decrease charges of tension and despair. Meaningful friendships provide a aid tool for the duration of hard times, contributing to better intellectual fitness.

4. Increased Happiness:

Positive Influence: Meaningful friendships contribute to happiness. Shared stories, laughter, and mutual know-how create a fantastic have an effect on that complements usual existence pleasure.

5. Enhanced Self-Esteem:

Validation and Support: Meaningful friendships offer validation and assist. Having pals who respect and help one's strengths and achievements boosts vanity and self notion.

6. Coping Mechanism:

Shared Coping Strategies: Meaningful friendships provide coping mechanisms in the course of traumatic situations. Friends offer numerous perspectives, advice, and a listening ear, helping people navigate difficulties with resilience.

7. Longevity and Physical Health:

Health Benefits: Meaningful friendships were associated with higher bodily health and durability. The emotional and social help from buddies surely affects elements like immune function and cardiovascular fitness.

eight. Stress Reduction:

Social Connection and Stress: Meaningful friendships lessen the physiological and mental effect of stress. Socializing with pals triggers the release of oxytocin, a hormone that promotes emotions of bonding and reduces strain.

nine. Improved Quality of Life:

Positive Impact on Well-Being: Meaningful friendships make a contribution to a complicated excellent of life. The satisfaction derived from shared reviews, celebrations, and ordinary moments provides richness and which means to existence.

10. Social Connectedness:

Sense of Purpose: Meaningful friendships foster a experience of purpose. The social connectedness derived from tremendous relationships gives human beings a reason to interact actively in life.

Chapter 8: Understanding College Life

College existence is a transformative journey, a rite of passage into maturity that is every exciting and daunting. It's the first step within the direction of independence, an opportunity to find out your passions, and a danger to form lifelong friendships. In this bankruptcy, we will delve into the crucial factors of know-how university existence as a way to manual you as a younger student. We'll discover a manner to conform to a trendy surroundings, appreciate the variety of university campuses, and recognize the not unusual social dynamics that form your enjoy.

1.1 Adapting to a New Environment

The Shift from High School to College

The transition from excessive college to college is a substantial one. For many, it's miles the primary time they have been far from domestic for an extended period, and it could be both exhilarating and difficult. In excessive university, you would possibly had been familiar collectively with your instructors, classmates, and the workout exercises of your each day lifestyles. College, however, is an entire new worldwide.

College campuses are regularly huge, extra numerous, and bustling with interest. You'll come upon a huge range of people from numerous backgrounds, which may be every interesting and intimidating. The instructional expectations are also higher, and you may have extra responsibility in your studying and each day lifestyles. It's vital to comply to this new environment to make the most of your college experience.

Tips for Adapting to College Life

1. Embrace Independence: College is a time to find out your independence. You'll have greater control over your schedule, coursework, and lifestyle choices. While this newfound freedom may be freeing, it additionally comes with the responsibility of making alternatives for your self. Embrace this independence with a experience of adulthood and responsibility.

2. Stay Organized: College life can get busy with schooling, assignments, and social sports activities. It's important to live organized to control some time efficiently. Use gear like planners, calendars, and apps to hold track of your schedule and assignments.

three. Seek Support: Don't hesitate to attempting to find help while wished. College campuses provide numerous belongings, inclusive of educational advisors, counseling offerings, and fitness facilities. Reach out to those belongings whilst managing academic, emotional, or private annoying conditions.

4. Get to Know Your Campus: Take the time to find out your college campus. Familiarize your self with the area of your commands, libraries, consuming halls, and specific important facilities. Knowing your manner spherical will reduce strain and help you sense extra at domestic.

five. Establish a Routine: While university existence can be spontaneous and severa, having a daily ordinary can provide balance.

Create a time table that permits you to balance teachers, social lifestyles, and self-care. A constant recurring can assist lessen strain and improve some time manage.

6. Make New Friends: College is an area to meet new people and gather friendships. Be open to forming connections together at the side of your buddies, roommates, and classmates. It's natural to revel in a piece apprehensive in the beginning, however bear in mind that everyone is inside the equal boat, attempting to find to make buddies.

1.2 The Diversity of College Campuses

One of the maximum extraordinary factors of college existence is the range you may come upon on campus. College campuses are regularly melting pots of cultures, backgrounds, and perspectives. It's an area wherein you could studies from individuals who come from superb additives of the sector and feature specific life studies. Embracing this variety is a key to private growth and a wealthy university revel in.

The Value of Diversity

Diversity in college is going far beyond really ethnicity and nationality. It consists of versions in race, gender, sexual orientation, socioeconomic backgrounds, and additional. This variety enriches the educational revel in through exposing you to a huge variety of perspectives and mind. It worrying conditions your preconceptions and broadens your statistics of the location.

Tips for Embracing Diversity

1. Cultural Curiosity: Approach humans from unique backgrounds with curiosity and a willingness to study. Ask questions, listen to their stories, and interact in conversations that assist you understand their subculture and studies better.

2. Participate in Multicultural Events: Most college campuses host multicultural occasions, fairs, and celebrations. Attend these sports to immerse your self in one-of-a-

type cultures, flavor numerous cuisines, and experience conventional performances.

three. Join Inclusive Clubs and Organizations: Many colleges have clubs and agencies that celebrate range and inclusivity. Joining such companies can be an remarkable manner to satisfy like-minded human beings and make contributions to building an inclusive campus community.

4. Challenge Stereotypes: Be aware about stereotypes and biases that would exist internal you. Challenge the ones preconceived notions and stereotypes and try to address anybody with equity and recognize.

5. Learn About Cultural Competence: Take gain of any workshops or guides associated with cultural competence and range. Understanding the dynamics of privilege, power, and oppression will can help you navigate complex problems.

1.Three Common Social Dynamics

Social dynamics in college may be complex and ever evolving. It's crucial to recognize the ones dynamics to navigate your social existence correctly and construct great relationships. Here are a few not unusual social dynamics you may come across:

Cliques and Friend Groups

In university, you'll be conscious that students often shape cliques or friend businesses based totally completely mostly on shared hobbies, pursuits, or instructional applications. These agencies provide a enjoy of belonging and assist. While they will be notable for constructing connections, it's also important to be open to assembly humans out of doors your immediately circle.

Extracurricular Activities

Participating in extracurricular sports together with clubs, sports activities sports, or student agencies is a extremely good way to fulfill individuals who percentage your interests. These sports activities provide a established surroundings for building friendships and pursuing your passions.

Networking and Academic Relationships

College is not pretty loads making friends; it is also about constructing expert relationships and networking. You'll interact with professors, mentors, and classmates who can offer precious guidance and opportunities in your future career.

Dorm Life

If you are dwelling on campus, dorm life can be a massive part of your social revel in. It's an environment in that you're in near proximity to special university students, and it's not unusual to form connections in conjunction with your roommates, floormates, and buddies.

Parties and Social Events

College often consists of parties, mixers, and diverse social sports. While they'll be amusing and a way to satisfy new people, it's far critical to navigate the ones settings responsibly and prioritize your safety and well-being.

Understanding those social dynamics will assist you adapt to university life extra efficiently and bring together a nicely-rounded social community. It's crucial to strike a balance amongst forming deep connections inside smaller organizations and increasing your social circle to encompass range. College life is an opportunity to discover, study, and develop, and know-how the dynamics of your new environment is step one towards a satisfying enjoy.

Building Confidence and Self-Esteem

College may be an thrilling but tough time in a more younger person's existence. It's a segment wherein you've got the possibility to analyze, broaden, and make lifelong friendships. However, to make the most of this revel in, it's miles important to increase the self warranty and vanity had to navigate the complexities of university existence. In this economic disaster, we're able to explore the essential elements of constructing self assurance and shallowness: growing a first rate self-picture, overcoming shyness and social anxiety, and setting practical expectancies.

2.1 Developing a Positive Self-Image

Understanding Self-Image

Your self-photograph is the intellectual image you've got had been given of your self. It's formed with the useful resource of your beliefs, testimonies, and perceptions of who you're. Developing a first rate self-image is a foundational step in building self belief and shallowness. When you note yourself in a great mild, it will become lots less complex to consider for your talents and engage with others extra with a piece of success.

Tips for Developing a Positive Self-Image

1. Practice Self-Compassion: Treat yourself with kindness and statistics. Just like clearly anybody else, you have got strengths and

weaknesses. Instead of dwelling on your flaws, reputation in your strengths and what makes you precise.

2. Challenge Negative Self-Talk: Pay interest to the manner you communicate to your self. Are you overly critical? Challenge awful self-speak via converting it with extra tremendous and provoking affirmations.

three. Accept Imperfection: It's critical to simply accept that no character is pleasant. Embrace your imperfections and recognize that they are part of what makes you human. Perfection is an improbable aim, and striving for it can result in vain strain.

4. Set Realistic Goals: Set achievable desires for yourself. When you advantage those dreams, you could assemble a revel in of fulfillment, which in flip bolsters your arrogance. Start with small, possible duties and grade by grade paintings your way as plenty as greater enormous demanding situations.

5. Surround Yourself with Positive People: Choose pals and buddies who uplift and aid you. Toxic relationships can erode your self-photo and self perception, so it is critical to cultivate a great and supportive social circle.

6. Seek Personal Growth: Engage in sports activities activities and hobbies that you are passionate about. The pursuit of private hobbies assist you to find out your strengths and abilties, boosting yourself-picture within the process.

7. Take Care of Your Physical Health: Eating nicely, exercise frequently, and getting enough sleep can considerably effect yourself-photograph. When you address your bodily health, you are much more likely to feel good about your self.

eight. Learn from Mistakes: Understand that making errors is a herbal a part of existence. Instead of living on failures, view them as possibilities for growth and studying. Every setback may be a steppingstone in the path of self-improvement.

2.2 Overcoming Shyness and Social Anxiety

Shyness vs. Social Anxiety

Shyness and social tension are common annoying conditions for hundreds college college students. It's important to apprehend the distinction between the 2:

Shyness is a natural character trait. Shy humans may additionally moreover revel in reserved or uncomfortable in positive social conditions, but it'd now not normally intervene with their every day lives.

Social anxiety, rather, is an immoderate fear of social conditions that could motive extensive distress. It can show up as physical symptoms and signs like sweating, a racing coronary coronary heart, or maybe panic assaults.

Tips for Overcoming Shyness and Social Anxiety

1. Gradual Exposure: If you're shy or socially stressful, begin via exposing your self to social

conditions gradually. Begin with small, low-stress interactions and paintings your way as an awful lot as greater tough ones.

2. Practice Active Listening: When carrying out conversations, awareness on being an lively listener. This can take the strain off you to constantly speak and could assist you to connect with others on a deeper degree.

3. Challenge Negative Thoughts: Social anxiety is regularly fueled through horrible mind and self-doubt. Challenge those thoughts thru analyzing their validity. Are your problems primarily based mostly on data, or are they exaggerated?

four. Relaxation Techniques: Learn and practice relaxation techniques like deep respiratory or meditation to control tension signs and signs and symptoms and signs. These machine may be priceless in lowering social anxiety.

five. Seek Professional Help: If social tension is substantially affecting your every day existence, undergo in thoughts searching out assist from a mental fitness expert. Therapy, which include cognitive-behavioral treatment, can be specially effective in addressing social anxiety.

6. Join Supportive Groups: Participate in social clubs or organizations that percentage your pastimes. Being with like-minded people could make social interactions greater comfortable and fun.

7. Set Realistic Goals: Don't anticipate your self to turn out to be a social butterfly in a single day. Set realistic, possible social desires, and have a good time your improvement, regardless of how small it could seem.

eight. Visualization and Positive Affirmations: Visualize your self in social situations, feeling assured and relaxed. Using excessive fine affirmations also can decorate your vanity and help you technique social interactions with a greater best mind-set.

2.Three Setting Realistic Expectations

The College Myth College is regularly portrayed within the media as a non-save you birthday party packed with fun and adventure. While university may be a tremendous and amusing enjoy, it is critical to technique it with sensible expectations. The "university fantasy" can bring about sadness if you count on every moment to be a wild celebration or an educational revelation.

Balancing Fun and Responsibility

In reality, college is a aggregate of every a laugh and obligation. You'll have interesting social reports, however you can moreover face academic demanding situations and duties. Setting practical expectancies way information that there might be times when you need to recognition to your research, attend education, and complete assignments.

Chapter 9: Finding Your Niche

College is an area of countless possibilities, and it offers a large number of opportunities to find out, examine, and develop. As a younger pupil enrolled in university, finding your area of interest is a important step in making the maximum of your university experience. In this bankruptcy, we are capable of dive into the numerous methods you could discover your place of hobby on campus, from exploring your interests and passions to becoming a member of clubs and agencies and appealing in sports activities activities and amusement sports.

3.1 Exploring Your Interests and Passions

Embracing Your Curiosity

College is a completely precise duration for your existence when you have the liberty to discover your pursuits and passions to the fullest. It's a time to growth your horizons, strive new things, and find out what simply excites you. Exploring your interests and passions is an vital step in finding your area of interest on campus.

Tips for Exploring Your Interests and Passions

1. Reflect on Your Hobbies: Think about the sports you loved in excessive college or throughout your loose time. These interests frequently suggest areas of interest that you may in addition discover in university.

2. Attend Introductory Classes: Many faculties offer introductory guides if you want to can help you dip your feet into severa topics. These training will can help you end up privy to areas of study or hobby that resonate with you.

three. Visit College Fairs and Exhibitions: Colleges often host festivals and exhibitions showcasing fantastic clubs, groups, and academic packages. Attend the ones occasions to get a pinnacle diploma view of the possibilities to be had.

four. Talk to Professors and Advisors: Professors and educational advisors can provide precious insights and steerage on ability regions of check that align together along with your pursuits. Don't hesitate to acquire out to them for recommendation.

5. Connect with Upperclassmen: Upperclassmen can offer precious advice based totally definitely mostly on their private studies. They can recommend clubs, businesses, or publications that align at the side of your hobbies.

6. Experiment and Be Open-Minded: Be open to attempting new matters, regardless of the reality that they fall outdoor your consolation sector. College is a time for experimentation, and you could find out new passions along the way.

7. Seek Mentorship: Find mentors or feature models who're professionals in fields that interest you. Their guidance can be instrumental in assisting you find out your passions and broaden your location of interest.

eight. Participate in Workshops and Seminars: Many schools offer workshops, seminars, and tourist speaker events. These can be superb opportunities to delve deeper into unique regions of hobby and connect to like-minded human beings.

3.2 Joining Clubs and Organizations

The Power of Clubs and Organizations

College campuses are teeming with clubs and organizations that cater to a large style of pastimes and passions. Joining those corporations may be a gateway to locating your location of hobby and forming huge connections with fellow college students who proportion your enthusiasm.

Tips for Joining Clubs and Organizations

1. Research and Explore: Research the golf equipment and agencies to be had for your campus. Attend membership fairs and statistics periods to investigate extra about them. Take be aware of those that pique your interest.

2. Consider Your Interests: Choose golf equipment and corporations that align along side your interests and passions. Whether it's miles related to a hobby, instructional venture, social cause, or cultural affinity, finding a fixed that resonates with you is top.

3. Start Small: Don't sense forced to join a dozen golf equipment right now. Begin with one or groups that simply hobby you. This permits you to certainly engage and make investments a while in a huge manner.

four. Attend Meetings and Events: Once you have got joined a membership or company, actively participate with the beneficial aid of attending conferences and activities. This is an superb manner to fulfill those who percent your interests and form connections.

5. Consider Leadership Roles: As you grow to be more concerned, do not forget taking up control roles inside the business enterprise. Being a part of the control group can deepen your involvement and assist you discover your area of interest even similarly.

6. Connect with Members: Build relationships with unique human beings. Attend social activities, collaborate on responsibilities, and get to recognise your fellow club or enterprise contributors on a personal diploma.

7. Balance Your Commitments: Be aware of a while and commitments. Ensure that your involvement in clubs and agencies does now not weigh down your educational obligations.

eight. Explore New Areas: While it's miles superb to sign up for golf equipment related to your present day pastimes, additionally endure in thoughts exploring new regions. Joining severa clubs can introduce you to at the least one-of-a-type studies and growth your horizons.

3.3 Sports and Recreational Activities

The Benefits of Physical Activity

Engaging in sports activities activities and enjoyment sports activities sports can be an great way to find out your area of interest in university. Not high-quality do these sports activities sell physical health, but in addition they provide a platform for social interaction, teamwork, and private increase.

Tips for Exploring Sports and Recreational Activities

1. Try Different Sports: Experiment with various sports activities activities and bodily sports. Whether it's traditional sports like football or basketball or opportunity activities like yoga or mountaineering, explore what fits you awesome.

2. Participate in Intramurals: Many faculties offer intramural sports, that are organized for college college students to compete in the campus community. Joining an intramural organization can be a amusing and coffee-pressure way to have interaction in sports activities activities.

three. Attend Open Gym or Fitness Classes: Visit the university fitness center or health club to find out unique exercising options. Many colleges provide corporation health education that may be a top notch manner to live energetic even as assembly new people.

4. Join Club Teams: If you are enthusiastic about a specific task, do not forget attempting out for a club team. These groups are frequently a whole lot much less competitive than varsity sports sports however offer a greater primarily based and organized experience.

five. Participate in Campus Events: Attend sports activities sports and tournaments organized thru your university. This can be an tremendous way to immerse yourself inside the sports activities sports lifestyle of your campus and connect with fellow lovers.

6. Challenge Yourself: As you've got interplay in sports activities sports activities and amusement sports, set private desires and worrying conditions. Pushing your physical limits may be a worthwhile manner to boom your talents and self assure.

7. Embrace Teamwork: If you take component in group sports sports sports, reputation on building teamwork competencies. Collaborating with others can beautify your social and management talents.

eight. Prioritize Health and Well-Being: While taking component in sports activities sports, undergo in mind to prioritize your health and nicely-being. Stay hydrated, placed on suitable protection machine, and take critical precautions to prevent accidents.

By exploring your hobbies and passions, becoming a member of golf equipment and organizations, and attractive in sports activitles sports and amusement sports activities, you could open doors to new reports and connections in college. These interests will no longer only assist you locate your area of interest but additionally contribute to your non-public boom and enhance your college adventure. Remember that university is a time to find out, find out, and shape your identity, and locating your area of interest is an essential a part of that approach.

Making the Most of Orientation Week

Orientation week is a pivotal and interesting period in a college scholar's life. It's the gateway for your university adventure, wherein you can have the possibility to find out the campus, meet new human beings, and make your self acquainted with the college surroundings. As a infant enrolled in university, this economic damage will guide you through making the most of your orientation week, overlaying techniques for a a success begin, the significance of icebreakers and networking activities, and forming those initial connections so that you can form your college enjoy.

four.1 Strategies for a Successful Orientation

The Importance of Orientation

Orientation week is your advent to university lifestyles. It's designed to help you transition into your new environment without difficulty, so making the most of it's miles important. A a success orientation will set the volume for a fulfilling and amusing university revel in.

Tips for a Successful Orientation

1. Prepare in Advance: Before your orientation week starts offevolved offevolved, evaluation the time desk, and make a listing of essential gadgets to convey. Being properly-prepared will help reduce any anxiety you may be feeling.

2. Attend All Sessions: Make certain to attend all orientation instructions and sports. These are designed to provide you with valuable statistics about the university, instructional packages, and help services available.

3. Ask Questions: Don't hesitate to ask questions. Orientation is the right time to clarify any doubts you can have. Whether it's miles about campus facilities, instructional requirements, or college rules, looking for answers will help you experience more assured.

four. Engage Actively: Be an lively participant in the course of orientation classes. Engage in discussions, share your thoughts, and take benefit of possibilities to interact with fellow college college college students.

5. Explore the Campus: Take time to discover the college campus. Familiarize yourself with the place of your lessons, libraries, consuming halls, and other vital facilities. Knowing your manner round will lessen pressure and assist you enjoy greater at domestic.

6. Meet Your Advisors: Your academic advisors and mentors are there to manual you. Use orientation as an possibility to meet them, speak your instructional goals, and are trying to find their advice.

7. Embrace Diversity: Orientation is a risk to meet humans from diverse backgrounds. Embrace this range and take the possibility to examine particular cultures and perspectives.

8. Be Open to New Experiences: During orientation, you'll be furnished with

possibilities to attempt new sports activities activities or be part of golf equipment and businesses. Be open to new reviews and do no longer be afraid to step from your consolation zone.

nine. Plan Your Schedule: Review your elegance time table and any extracurricular sports activities you need to sign up for. Planning a while efficiently will assist you stay organized and balance your academic and social commitments.

10. Stay Hydrated and Rested: Orientation week can be busy, so make certain to stay hydrated and get sufficient rest. Your well-being is important for a a success start to university life.

4.2 Icebreakers and Networking Events

Breaking the Ice

Icebreakers and networking occasions are an crucial a part of orientation week. These sports activities activities are designed to help you get to understand your fellow students and create a experience of network. While they'll appear a chunk intimidating in advance than the whole thing, they may be truly a fun and treasured way to form connections.

The Importance of Icebreakers and Networking

Icebreakers and networking events serve severa features:

They assist you meet new human beings and shape preliminary connections.

They foster a experience of belonging and network on campus.

They introduce you to capability friends, test partners, and aid systems.

They encourage you to extend communique and social abilties.

Tips for Participating in Icebreakers and Networking Events

1. Be Approachable: Approach those activities with an open and pleasant mind-set. Smile,

make eye touch, and be approachable to others in search of to connect.

2. Introduce Yourself: Don't appearance in advance to others to provoke introductions. Take step one thru introducing your self to people you meet. Share your call, wherein you are from, and what you are studying.

3. Listen Actively: When assignment conversations, practice lively listening. Pay interest to what others are announcing, ask questions, and display a real hobby of their memories and stories.

4. Share About Yourself: Be willing to percent about your very very own interests, hobbies, and evaluations. This can spark commonplace floor for conversation and construct connections.

five. Participate in Group Activities: Join institution sports activities and video video video games. These sports activities are designed to inspire interaction and teamwork, making it much less hard to connect with others.

6. Exchange Contact Information: If you meet a person you hook up with, do not hesitate to trade contact records. This may be the muse for destiny interactions and friendships.

7. Attend Various Events: Attend a number of icebreakers and networking activities. This will will allow you to meet particular human beings with numerous pursuits and backgrounds.

Chapter 10: Effective Communication Skills

Effective conversation is a critical capability that plays a important characteristic in every element of life, and university is not any exception. As a toddler enrolled in university, you may come upon a diverse array of people and situations that require powerful conversation. In this financial ruin, we are able to discover 4 important additives of effective communication capabilities: lively listening, nonverbal conversation, communication starters and icebreakers, and handling war and tough conversations.

five.1 Active Listening

The Art of Listening

Active listening is a critical detail of powerful communique. It consists of no longer honestly hearing terms however additionally information, processing, and responding to the speaker in a extremely good way. Whether you are in a classroom, social putting, or agency task, lively listening is a information that allow you to collect relationships and prevail academically.

Tips for Active Listening

1. Give Your Full Attention: When a person is speakme, deliver them your entire interest. Put away distractions, make eye touch, and attention on what they may be pronouncing.

2. Avoid Interrupting: Let the speaker end their thoughts in advance than responding. Interrupting can disrupt the go with the flow of the communication and make the speaker experience unheard.

3. Ask Clarifying Questions: If you are unsure approximately some component, do no longer hesitate to ask for explanation. This no longer best shows that you're engaged within the verbal exchange but additionally enables you apprehend the speaker's perspective higher.

four. Use Nonverbal Cues: Nonverbal cues, which includes nodding or smiling, can signal which you're actively listening and provoking the speaker to maintain.

5. Reflect and Summarize: After the speaker has finished, mirror on what they have got stated and summarize their main elements. This shows which you've been attentive and comprehended their message.

6. Empathize: Try to put yourself within the speaker's shoes and understand their feelings and perspective. Empathy is a powerful tool for building rapport.

7. Avoid Formulating a Response While Listening: It's commonplace to think about a manner to reply on the equal time as a person is speakme. However, it may restriction your capability to pay interest actively. Focus on information first, and then formulate your response.

eight. Practice Patience: Not each communique may have a quick and simple preference. Practice persistence, in particular in complex or emotionally charged discussions.

five.2 Nonverbal Communication

The Power of Nonverbal Cues

Nonverbal verbal exchange encompasses gestures, facial expressions, body language, and tone of voice. It's a effective form of verbal exchange that could frequently communicate louder than terms. Being aware about your private nonverbal cues and spotting them in others can beautify your ability to hold and interpret messages efficiently.

Tips for Understanding and Using Nonverbal Communication

1. Maintain Eye Contact: In many cultures, keeping appropriate eye touch is a sign of attentiveness and admire. However, take word not to stare, as this can make others uncomfortable.

2. Gestures and Body Language: Pay interest for your very own gestures and body language, in addition to those of the humans you are interacting with. Be aware of your posture and facial expressions.

three. Tone of Voice: The tone in which you communicate can deliver masses of facts. Practice speaking in a smooth, friendly, and respectful tone to beautify your conversation.

four. Space and Proximity: Different cultures and people have numerous consolation zones on the venture of personal area. Be privy to this and adjust your physical proximity because of this.

5. Use Mirroring: Mirroring, or matching a person's nonverbal cues, can create a feel of connection and statistics. However, use this technique subtly and respectfully.

6. Watch for Incongruence: Sometimes, someone's nonverbal cues may not align with their terms. If you enjoy incongruence, it can be nicely surely really worth exploring further

to apprehend their real emotions or intentions.

7. Emphasize Active Listening: Nonverbal cues, which include nodding and retaining eye contact, can decorate your energetic listening competencies. They show that you're engaged within the verbal exchange.

eight. Control Your Nervous Habits: We all have apprehensive conduct, like fidgeting or tapping our toes. Recognize these behavior and try to control them at the same time as engaged in important conversations.

5.Three Conversation Starters and Icebreakers

Initiating Conversations

Starting a verbal exchange, mainly with a person you don't know nicely, can be tough. Conversation starters and icebreakers are treasured tool so one can permit you to initiate and keep substantial conversations. Whether you're assembly new pals, networking, or interacting with professors, having a few communication starters up your sleeve can be pretty reachable.

Tips for Effective Conversation Starters and Icebreakers

1. Ask Open-Ended Questions: Instead of asking sure-or-no questions, pose open-ended ones that invite greater extended responses. For instance, "What do you revel in doing in your unfastened time?" in location of "Do you want sports?"

2. Compliments and Observations: Offering a reward or making an declaration about your environment may be an brilliant communication starter. For example, "I love your backpack! Where did you get it?" or "The campus library has a tremendous view, does not it?"

three. Share Your Own Experiences: Sharing a private anecdote can harm the ice and encourage the opportunity person to do the identical. For example, "I had the most brilliant pizza at a nearby joint closing night time time. Do you experience trying out new locations to devour?"

4. Common Interests: If you understand you percentage a common hobby, use it as a communication starter. For instance, "I heard you are into photographs. I love taking photographs too. Do you have got were given a fave trouble to picture?"

five. Recent News or Events: Discussing cutting-edge facts or occasions, together with a huge campus taking place or a trending issue keep in mind, can provide a relevant and tasty location to begin for a communique.

6. Focusing at the Other Person: Show actual hobby within the other character through manner of asking about their heritage, studies, and pursuits. People appreciate while you take the time to get to understand them.

7. Light Humor: A little little bit of moderate humor may be an superb icebreaker. Sharing a funny tale or a mild humorous tale can help damage anxiety and make people feel cushty.

8. Practice Active Listening: As the opportunity individual responds in your icebreaker, actively pay attention to their answers and ask study-up questions. This continues the communication flowing.

5.Four Handling Conflict and Difficult Conversations

Conflict Resolution

College lifestyles isn't with out its conflicts and hard conversations. Whether it is a battle of phrases with a roommate, a miscommunication with a professor, or problems inside a group undertaking, learning a manner to take care of battle and tough conversations is critical for a a achievement college experience.

Tips for Handling Conflict and Difficult Conversations

1. Stay Calm and Collected: When faced with struggle, live calm and collected. Emotional reactions can extend the state of affairs and save you inexperienced verbal exchange.

2. Choose the Right Time and Place: Find the suitable time and region to address the problem. Ensure privateness and minimum distractions to popularity on the communique.

three. Use "I" Statements: Express your thoughts and emotions using "I" statements. For example, say, "I felt annoyed even as..." in location of creating accusatory statements.

4. Active Listening: In war resolution, energetic listening is important. Give the other party an possibility to precise their attitude and worries without interruption.

five. Seek Common Ground: Look for areas of agreement and common desires to assemble a basis for resolving the battle.

6. Find Solutions Together: Approach the conversation with the aim of locating solutions together. Brainstorm mind and do not forget compromises.

7. Stay Respectful: Regardless of the disagreement, hold a deferential and

courteous tone sooner or later of the verbal exchange.

eight. Consider Mediation: If the conflict proves difficult to remedy independently, don't forget associated with a mediator, which includes a resident consultant, professor, or campus counselor, to assist facilitate the communicate.

9. Learn from the Experience: Even difficult conversations can provide treasured training. Reflect on the experience and remember how you may enhance your verbal exchange capabilities and prevent similar conflicts inside the destiny.

10. Forgive and Move Forward: After a decision has been reached, it's far vital to forgive and pass ahead. Holding onto grudges can prevent your college experience and relationships.

Effective verbal exchange abilities, which consist of lively listening, nonverbal communication, conversation starters and icebreakers, and battle selection, are beneficial device for navigating college existence successfully. These capabilities will help you shape massive connections, specific your thoughts and thoughts, and clear up conflicts constructively. Remember that powerful communique is a capacity that can be continuously developed and delicate, and it performs a pivotal characteristic for your personal and academic growth in the course of your college adventure.

Dorm Life and Roommates

Living in a dormitory at some point of your college years is a totally precise and transformative revel in. It's a time while you transition from the comforts of domestic to a shared dwelling region, regularly with roommates. In this bankruptcy, we are going to discover the dynamic global of dorm existence and roommates, defensive the specialists and cons of residing inside the dorms, the artwork of constructing high quality relationships with roommates, and the possibilities to engage in dormitory social existence.

6.1 Living in the Dorms: Pros and Cons

Pros of Dorm Life

Living in a university dormitory gives a number of blessings:

1. Convenience: Dorms are normally located on or near the campus, making it available to wait instructions, get proper of access to the library, and take part in campus sports.

2. Community: You're a part of a near-knit community in that you are probably to fulfill new friends, have a study partners, or even future lifelong connections.

3. Independence: Dorm existence gives a taste of independence. You'll have the freedom to govern it slow desk, make choices approximately your each day ordinary, and revel in a sense of self-sufficiency.

4. Resource Access: Dorms regularly offer sources like laundry centers, common areas,

and study regions, making it less hard to stability your educational and social existence.

5. Experience Diversity: Dormitories house university students from numerous backgrounds and cultures, fostering an environment of range and multicultural interactions.

6. Extracurricular Activities: Many dorms installation social sports, workshops, and packages that provide possibilities for personal growth and amusement.

Cons of Dorm Life

While dorm life gives many advantages, it moreover comes with its set of demanding situations:

1. Limited Privacy: Sharing a room or living area with roommates manner decreased privacy. It may additionally take time to regulate to having someone spherical constantly.

2. Noise and Distractions: Dorms may be noisy and busy places, making it hard to find out a quiet vicinity for reading or relaxation.

three. Conflict with Roommates: Differences in existence and conduct can motive conflicts with roommates. Learning to speak and compromise is important.

four. Shared Facilities: Common facilities, together with toilets and kitchens, can emerge as crowded and require coordination with one-of-a-type dorm residents.

five. Rules and Regulations: Dorms have guidelines and regulations to preserve order and safety. Adhering to the ones guidelines is essential.

6. Limited Space: Dorm rooms are generally small, requiring modern area management.

6.2 Building Relationships with Roommates

The Roommate Dynamic

Sharing your residing place with roommates is an essential part of dorm existence. Building powerful relationships together with your roommates is crucial for developing a harmonious and fun residing environment. Here are some strategies to foster suitable relationships along with your roommates:

1. Communicate Openly: Effective communication is the muse of a wholesome roommate dating. Discuss expectations, barriers, and concerns openly and genuinely.

2. Set Ground Rules: Establish ground tips and barriers that everybody can agree on. This may embody quiet hours, cleanliness expectations, and sharing obligations.

3. Respect Differences: Understand that your roommates might also have particular conduct, schedules, and lifestyles. Respect these versions and be inclined to compromise.

4. Privacy: Everyone goals their privateness. Be respectful of your roommates' want for personal location and barriers.

five. Conflict Resolution: Conflicts are inevitable in shared dwelling areas. Learn to cope with conflicts constructively via the usage of using actively listening, knowledge every extraordinary's views, and finding solutions collectively.

6. Shared Responsibilities: Collaborate on shared obligations, which includes cleansing, looking for groceries, and looking after communal regions. Fairly distribute responsibilities to keep away from resentment.

7. Support Each Other: Be there to your roommates at some point of each difficult and thrilled times. Offering guide and expertise can supply a boost in your bond.

8. Roommate Agreements: Some colleges offer roommate agreements or contracts that define expectations and responsibilities. These can be valuable device for clarity.

nine. Build Connections: Make an try to construct connections together together with your roommates through spending time together, sharing food, and participating in dormitory sports.

10. Be Mindful of Noise: Be aware of your noise level and its impact on your roommates. Use headphones, study in certain quiet areas, and admire quiet hours.

6.Three Engaging in Dormitory Social Life

Dormitory Communities

Dormitories are extra than in truth residing spaces; they're vibrant corporations wherein you can have interaction in social sports activities activities and shape lasting connections. Here's the manner to make the maximum of dormitory social existence:

Chapter 11: Attending Social Events

Social activities are a colorful and critical part of the college revel in. They provide opportunities to make new friends, assemble a social community, and create lasting reminiscences. In this chapter, we will find out the numerous sorts of social activities you can come across in college, which consist of parties, mixers, and gatherings. We'll also speak the way to make the maximum of campus activities and provide hints for effective networking at those gatherings.

7.1 Parties, Mixers, and Gatherings

Embracing the College Social Scene

College is not pretty tons lecturers; it is a time to encompass a colourful social scene. Parties, mixers, and gatherings are not unusual furniture in university existence, presenting a platform for university students to unwind, socialize, and shape connections.

Parties

Parties are frequently informal and snug gatherings wherein university college college students come together to rejoice, have fun, and experience every special's corporation. Whether it's far a party, a themed event, or a spontaneous get-collectively, activities offer a harm from the academic routine and a threat to let loose.

Mixers

Mixers are activities designed to deliver tremendous agencies of human beings collectively, usually for the purpose of mingling and socializing. These occasions may be prepared by golf equipment, instructional departments, or student agencies and frequently have a particular subject matter or hobby, collectively with a primary or shared interest.

Gatherings

Gatherings can be whatever from casual hangouts in a dorm room to potluck dinners with buddies. They offer a comfortable putting for socializing, communication, and constructing connections. Gatherings may be a super manner to foster a feel of community and make stronger friendships.

7.2 Making the Most of Campus Events

Engaging with Campus Life

College campuses are buzzing with severa occasions and sports activities that cater to a big sort of interests and passions. Engaging with campus sports is a exceptional manner to supplement your university revel in and make bigger your social circle.

Attend Sporting Events

Many colleges have their sports activities sports sports agencies and host domestic video video games or suits. Attending the ones occasions can be a thrilling and active manner to aid your college, bond with fellow college college students, and enjoy the pride of sports.

Explore Cultural Events

Colleges frequently host cultural occasions, which incorporates track stay suggests, art work exhibitions, dance performances, and more. These activities can introduce you to new art office work, cultures, and views, making them each academic and a laugh.

Join Clubs and Organizations

College campuses are home to a plethora of clubs and corporations, each imparting unique sports and possibilities. Joining those companies now not best lets in you to discover your pursuits but moreover hook up with like-minded folks who percent your passions.

Attend Workshops and Seminars

Colleges frequently host workshops, seminars, and vacationer speaker occasions. These provide valuable possibilities to decorate your statistics and abilties at the equal time as networking with experts to your situation of interest.

Participate in Volunteer Activities

Getting involved in volunteer and network company sports sports will let you deliver decrease back to the network and meet others who percent your determination to social reasons.

Celebrate Campus Traditions

Many colleges have longstanding traditions, which include homecoming, spirit weeks, and cultural celebrations. Engaging within the ones traditions can foster a sense of belonging and provide fun and fantastic reviews.

7.Three Tips for Networking at Social Functions

The Art of Networking

Networking at social capabilities is an critical talent this is going beyond truely making friends. It includes constructing connections with buddies, professors, and experts who will assist you to to your educational and destiny career endeavors. Here are a few suggestions for effective networking at social abilties:

1. Be Approachable: Approachability is excessive to networking. Smile, make eye contact, and appear open to communication.

2. Introduce Yourself: Don't watch for others to provoke introductions. Take the first step through introducing your self, sharing your call, and inquiring for theirs.

3. Prepare a Brief Introduction: Have a concise self-introduction prepared, highlighting your name, primary, and a quick precis of your hobbies or goals.

four. Active Listening: Actively pay attention while undertaking conversations. Show a right hobby inside the different individual's mind and reminiscences.

five. Ask Questions: Asking questions about the alternative man or woman's historic beyond, critiques, and goals may be a first-rate way to connect and look at greater approximately them.

6. Share Your Interests: Share your pursuits and dreams at the same time as applicable to the conversation. It can spark connections with those who have similar aspirations.

7. Follow Up: After an initial meeting, keep in mind to comply with up with the humans you have got met. Send a nice message or invite them to connect on social media.

8. Business Cards and Contact Information: If appropriate, exchange contact data or business enterprise playing gambling cards. This can facilitate future networking and collaboration.

nine. Dress Appropriately: Dressing accurately for the event might also want to make a pleasant impact on others. It's important to be presentable and snug.

10. Be Respectful and Professional: Maintain a respectful and professional demeanor within the route of networking activities. This consists of being punctual, honoring

commitments, and treating others courteously.

11. Diversity Matters: Be open to networking with people from severa backgrounds and fields of examine. You in no manner apprehend in which treasured connections may additionally moreover come from.

12. Attend Multiple Events: Don't restriction your networking to simply one occasion. Attend an entire lot of social capabilities and sports activities to increase your community.

thirteen. Elevator Pitch: Craft a quick and impactful elevator pitch that concisely describes your dreams and interests. This can be a to be had device for networking.

Networking is an ongoing gadget that could purpose opportunities for mentorship, collaboration, and destiny career prospects. Effective networking includes now not satisfactory making connections however additionally nurturing and keeping them over the years. By training the ones tips, you may navigate social functions with confidence and assemble a strong community that allows you to serve you well within the course of your university years and past.

In college, attending social events, whether it is events, mixers, or gatherings, offers a useful possibility to socialize, create memories, and increase your community. Embrace the social scene, engage with campus activities, and practice the paintings of effective networking to make the maximum of your university enjoy. Remember that building connections and growing a colorful social life can beautify your private boom and open doorways to exciting opportunities all through your college adventure.

Study Groups and Academic Connections

Your adventure thru college isn't always absolutely about educational analyzing; it is also a time to foster significant connections collectively along side your buddies and professors. In this financial ruin, we're going to find out the significance of look at agencies, how they'll be able to result in lasting friendships, the blessings of partnering with classmates on educational tasks, and the use of office hours now not handiest for instructional help however additionally to bring together relationships alongside side your professors.

eight.1 Leveraging Study Groups for Friendship

Building Bonds Through Study

Study companies are an vital a part of university lifestyles, offering an street for collaborative gaining knowledge of and know-how sharing. They serve a twin motive: no longer best do they enhance your expertise of route materials, but similarly they offer a totally specific possibility to shape lasting friendships alongside side your fellow university students.

Shared Academic Goals

One of the primary motives' college college students be part of have a study groups is to cope with hard coursework collaboratively. Sharing your academic goals and struggles with others can create a enjoy of camaraderie and brotherly love.

Enhanced Learning Experience

In a look at institution, you've got the gain of numerous views and techniques to learning. Engaging in discussions and debates can deepen your statistics of the challenge bear in mind.

Division of Workload

Study groups can be specially beneficial even as tackling large tasks or getting ready for checks. By dividing the workload and sharing responsibilities, you can lessen pressure and decorate overall performance.

Creating a Support System

Study organizations offer emotional assist at some point of annoying instructional durations. Sharing successes and annoying situations collectively collectively together with your peers can foster a sturdy manual tool.

Forming Lifelong Friendships

The connections you are making in take a look at organizations regularly expand past lecturers. Many college college students have met their closest pals via the ones collaborative mastering studies.

Tips for Leveraging Study Groups for Friendship

1. Be Open and Approachable: Approach take a look at employer conferences with an open and satisfactory mind-set. Create an inviting and inclusive surroundings.

2. Get to Know Your Peers: Take the time to get to understand your test employer people. Ask about their pastimes, interests, and aspirations outside of instructors.

three. Schedule Social Time: Plan occasional social gatherings together with your test corporation outside of tutorial settings. This allows you to bond on a personal degree.

four. Share Your Knowledge: Sharing your educational insights and notes can show off your willingness to assist your buddies, fostering a experience of reciprocity.

five. Be Supportive: Offer manual and encouragement in your have a examine organization individuals during tough times. A supportive thoughts-set can pork up your bonds.

6. Celebrate Achievements: Celebrate your collective successes, each big and small. Recognize and renowned every different's accomplishments.

7. Stay Connected Beyond Classes: Continue your relationships with test enterprise participants even after the splendor or semester has ended. Friendships can expand more potent over the years.

eight.2 Partnering with Classmates

Collaborative Academic Endeavors

Collaboration with classmates on instructional duties and assignments can be a profitable revel in. While it lets in distribute the workload, it furthermore gives a danger to investigate out of your pals and increase precious academic connections.

Different Perspectives

Working with classmates exposes you to severa views and strategies to hassle-solving. This range can reason richer and more complete instructional tasks.

Skill Development

Collaborative projects often require teamwork, communication, and business enterprise. These are critical abilities that you can boom on the identical time as partnering together with your peers.

Building Relationships

Working carefully with classmates on academic responsibilities affords opportunities to build relationships and friendships based on a shared dedication to excellence.

Networking

The connections you are making for the duration of collaborative tasks can amplify past the lecture room. Your friends also can end up valuable contacts for destiny career opportunities and networking.

A Sense of Accomplishment

Completing hard academic duties with the useful resource and contribution of your classmates can foster a feel of fulfillment and pride.

Tips for Partnering with Classmates

1. Choose Your Partners Wisely: Select companions primarily based completely mostly on their competencies, willpower, and compatibility along side your operating style. A nicely-matched group is much more likely to achieve success.

2. Establish Clear Roles: Define each crew member's responsibilities and roles inside the enterprise. This clarity facilitates prevent misunderstandings and conflicts.

three. Communicate Effectively: Maintain open and powerful conversation inside the institution. Regular updates and discussions are vital for project success.

4. Set Realistic Goals: Establish practical desires and timelines for your duties. This ensures which you're heading within the right direction to fulfill remaining dates and expectations.

5. Leverage Everyone's Strengths: Capitalize on every group member's strengths and information. This no longer most effective enhances the brilliant of the challenge however moreover builds a enjoy of apprehend amongst employer individuals.

6. Provide Constructive Feedback: Offer positive and respectful remarks to your pals.

Constructive grievance can result in development and growth.

7. Celebrate Achievements: Acknowledge and have fun milestones and accomplishments within the route of the assignment. Recognizing hard artwork can inspire the institution.

eight. Maintain Professionalism: Approach collaborative initiatives with professionalism and appreciate for your companions. Treat every brilliant with courtesy and attention.

eight.Three Using Office Hours for More Than Just Academics

Building Connections with Professors

Office hours are an underutilized beneficial aid for college university university college students. While they may be normally supposed for educational assist, moreover they provide a treasured possibility to construct relationships along with your professors. Here's the way to make the maximum of this possibility.

Seek Clarification

Utilize workplace hours to are looking for rationalization on route substances, assignments, and educational issues. This demonstrates your commitment on your studies and your interest within the issue depend.

Ask About Their Research

Many professors are actively engaged in research obligations. Inquire about their studies interests and tasks, showing real interest of their paintings.

Chapter 12: Online And Virtual Friendships

In trendy digital age, the landscape of friendship and social connections has elevated beyond the confines of in-individual interactions. Online and digital friendships have emerge as an essential a part of the college enjoy. In this monetary spoil, we will delve into the arena of on-line groups, the artwork of constructing massive relationships in virtual areas, and the significance of locating a stability among online and in-person socializing.

9.1 Exploring Online Communities

The Digital Social Universe

Online groups are virtual areas in which like-minded people come together to talk about common pursuits, percentage opinions, and construct connections. These organizations are diverse and a long way-mission, and they provide a completely unique opportunity to find out your passions and meet people from all around the global.

Types of Online Communities

1. Social Media Platforms: Social media networks like Facebook, Instagram, Twitter, and TikTok function areas where you may connect to pals, study influencers, and be part of businesses associated with your pursuits.

2. Forums and Message Boards: Online boards and message forums, which encompass Reddit, provide areas for in-depth discussions on a huge form of subjects.

3. Gaming Communities: Online gaming organizations supply game enthusiasts together to play, compete, and chat with fellow lovers.

4. Special Interest Groups: Various websites and structures cater to vicinity of interest hobbies, collectively with fan boards, hobbyist companies, and expert networks.

five. Virtual Worlds: Some platforms, like Second Life and VRChat, create digital worlds in which customers ought to have interplay with avatars and find out new environments.

Benefits of Online Communities

Global Connections: Online communities damage down geographical limitations, permitting you to connect to human beings from round the world.

Ease of Access: These structures are available 24/7, making it smooth to connect to others each time it's far reachable for you.

Niche Interests: Online agencies cater to unique pursuits, making sure you discover a employer of folks who share your passions.

Learning Opportunities: Engaging in discussions and sports inner those communities may be academic and provide opportunities for private growth.

Diverse Perspectives: Interacting with people from severa backgrounds can expand your thoughts-set and introduce you to new thoughts.

Tips for Exploring Online Communities

1. Choose Platforms Wisely: Select systems that align collectively together with your hobbies and values. Different communities have particular atmospheres and cultures.

2. Observe and Lurk: Before actively collaborating, take time to test and understand the network dynamics and etiquette.

three. Be Respectful: Treat others with recognize, even in on line spaces. Be aware of the impact of your phrases and actions.

4. Participate Actively: Engage in discussions, proportion your mind, and make a contribution to the network. Active participation fosters connections.

five. Maintain Privacy: Be careful about sharing non-public statistics on-line. Protect your privateness and use pseudonyms if crucial.

6. Stay Informed: Keep up with the rules and suggestions of the community to make sure you're in compliance.

7. Be Patient: Building connections in on line groups can take time. Be affected individual and allow relationships to broaden certainly.

nine.2 Building Meaningful Relationships Virtually

Nurturing Virtual Friendships

Virtual friendships, like in-character relationships, require try, receive as proper with, and communique. Whether you've got met a person in a web community or through virtual classes, proper right here's a way to assemble and maintain giant virtual relationships.

Establish Trust

Trust is the muse of any friendship. Be reliable, honest, and respectful in your interactions with digital pals.

Maintain Consistent Communication

Regular communique is important for virtual friendships. Consistently messaging or scheduling digital meetups can maintain the relationship sturdy.

Share Personal Stories and Experiences

Opening up approximately your existence, opinions, and challenges can help deepen your connection with virtual pals. It's a way to construct take transport of as true with and show vulnerability.

Celebrate Achievements and Milestones

Acknowledge and function an high-quality time each one in every of a type's successes, whether or no longer they will be academic, personal, or professional. Recognizing achievements can pork up your bond.

Problem-Solve Together

Navigating traumatic conditions and resolving conflicts is a part of any friendship. Approach troubles openly and collaboratively to discover answers.

Virtual Meetups

Arrange digital meetups through video calls or on-line video video games to spend amazing time together with your digital buddies. It's a way to create shared stories.

Stay in Touch Beyond the Screen

While digital verbal exchange is essential, staying in touch out of doors the digital international can be valuable. Send letters, care programs, or small surprises to expose your appreciation.

Overcoming Challenges

Virtual friendships include precise disturbing conditions, but with try and records, you may triumph over them:

Time Zone Differences: If your buddies are in brilliant time zones, coordinate your schedules and installation regular trap-up times.

Technology Hiccups: Technical issues can disrupt virtual verbal exchange. Be affected person and know-how after they rise up.

Miscommunication: In the absence of nonverbal cues, misunderstandings can upward thrust up. Be smooth in your conversation and ask for clarification at the same time as wanted.

Fading Connections: Virtual friendships can every so often fade due to loss of everyday communication. Make an try to preserve the connection.

Balancing In-Person and Virtual Friendships: Finding the proper balance among virtual and in-man or woman friendships may be difficult. Prioritize relationships primarily based in your desires and pursuits.

nine.Three Balancing Online and In-Person Socializing

Finding the Right Balance

Balancing online and in-character socializing is vital to a nicely-rounded university revel in. While on line connections provide consolation and a numerous social landscape, in-man or woman interactions provide a tangible and immediate experience of connection.

Benefits of In-Person Socializing

Emotional Connection: In-character interactions frequently bring about a more potent emotional connection because of face-to-face verbal exchange.

Physical Presence: Sharing physical region with friends permits for shared sports activities sports, like going to activities, exploring new places, and taking part in shared food.

Immediate Feedback: In-character interactions provide immediately feedback via frame language and facial expressions, primary to extra nuanced conversation.

Building Local Connections: In-character socializing enables you assemble connections with individuals for your close by community, which may be beneficial for networking and personal increase.

Benefits of Online Socializing

Global Reach: Online friendships can join you with humans global, introducing you to various views and thoughts.

Convenience: Virtual interactions are available, allowing you to connect with friends regardless of geographical distance.

Varied Interests: Online businesses cater to a wonderful sort of hobbies, making sure you discover a collection of like-minded individuals.

Flexibility: Virtual friendships offer flexibility in scheduling and allow for communique at your very very own tempo.

Tips for Balancing Online and In-Person Socializing

1. Prioritize Face-to-Face Interactions: While online pals are precious, take the time to prioritize in-individual interactions with friends you could meet regionally.

2. Set Boundaries: Manage some time with the aid of putting barriers between on-line and in-individual socializing. Create a time desk that balances each.

three. Regular Check-Ins: Maintain ordinary communique with every online and in-person friends to ensure no connections are ignored.

4. Blend Online and Offline Activities: Participate in on-line and offline sports collectively together along with your buddies, fostering connections in each geographical regions.

five. Consider Your Needs: Reflect in your social wishes and possibilities. Some people thrive with a aggregate of online and in-person interactions, even as others also can select one over the opportunity.

6. Be Mindful of Screen Time: Keep a watch fixed to your show show screen time to keep away from overindulging in digital socializing to the detriment of your well-being.

Balancing online and in-character socializing is a private adventure. It's critical to evaluate your desires, control a while successfully, and nurture connections in each nation-states to enjoy a properly-rounded and fun college experience.

Online and digital friendships have become an fundamental a part of the university enjoy, increasing your social horizons beyond the physical campus. Exploring online groups, building significant relationships in digital regions, and finding the right balance amongst on-line and in-man or woman socializing are all vital factors of navigating this digital era of friendship. By embracing the ones possibilities and training the pointers provided, you can create wealthy and severa social lifestyles that complements your university adventure.

Chapter 13: Maintaining And Nurturing Friendships

Maintaining and nurturing friendships is a essential ability to grasp during your college years. While making new friends is an interesting part of the university revel in, it's miles similarly vital to foster and preserve the relationships you have got constructed. In this chapter, we are able to delve into the artwork of comply with-up and consistency, discover the dynamics of dealing with friendships through the years, and equip you with strategies for battle decision and tackling hard conversations.

10.1 The Art of Follow-Up and Consistency

Cultivating Lasting Connections

Creating lasting and significant friendships requires ongoing try to willpower. The art work of follow-up and consistency performs a large position in nurturing relationships.

Stay in Touch

Friendship isn't a one-time event however an ongoing journey. Staying in contact through ordinary verbal exchange is crucial to keep the relationship sturdy.

Make Plans

Actively plan and time table sports together together with your pals. Whether it's miles a film night time time, a observe session, or a coffee date, the ones deliberate encounters solidify your bond.

Celebrate Milestones

Acknowledging and celebrating essential milestones in your friends' lives, collectively with birthdays, achievements, or existence activities, shows your assist and care.

Offer Support

During tough instances, provide your aid and a listening ear. Being there in your pals once they need you can deepen your connection.

Reciprocity

Friendship need to be a -way avenue. Be willing to give as a good deal as you obtain and hold a enjoy of balance in the dating.

Consistent Communication

Regular and steady communication is vital. Whether thru cellular phone calls, text messages, or face-to-face interactions, take some time to connect regularly.

Be Thoughtful

Small acts of thoughtfulness, like sending a kind message or a wonder present, can cross a long way in nurturing your friendships.

Be Patient

Friendships amplify and evolve over the years. Be affected character and permit your relationships to increase without a doubt and at their very personal pace.

Tips for Maintaining Consistency in Friendships

1. Set Reminders: Use virtual reminders or apps to prompt you to collect out and connect to your pals frequently.

2. Create Traditions: Establish traditions or wearing events that you may percent together along with your friends, whether or not or no longer or no longer it's far a weekly movie night time or an annual trekking journey.

three. Stay Engaged: Actively interact for your friends' lives. Ask approximately their testimonies and display a actual hobby in their reminiscences.

4. Practice Active Listening: When your pals percent their thoughts and feelings, exercising lively paying attention to in fact apprehend and empathize with their research.

5. Quality Over Quantity: Focus at the pleasant of your interactions instead of the amount. Meaningful and actual connections are more valuable than superficial ones.

6. Prioritize Face-to-Face Time: Whenever possible, prioritize face-to-face interactions, as they often cause deeper and further memorable connections.

10.2 Handling Friendships Over Time

The Evolution of Friendships

Friendships, like every different relationships, go through modifications and evolutions over time. Understanding the dynamics of managing friendships as they development is vital for their sturdiness.

Life Transitions

Throughout university and beyond, you and your friends will experience numerous lifestyles transitions, which incorporates converting majors, internships, and post-graduation plans. These transitions can have an effect on the dynamics of your friendships.

Prioritization

As you and your friends pursue specific desires and interests, you may need to prioritize a while and strength. This would possibly not suggest neglecting your friendships but alternatively locating a stability that allows you to help each different's aspirations.

Distance

Some friendships can be challenged by way of the use of geographical distance. When pals flow into away for task possibilities or particular motives, keeping the relationship can require greater try.

Changing Interests

Your interests and pursuits might also evolve over time. Embrace those changes, and if your pursuits diverge from your pals', it is an possibility to discover new passions at the same time as retaining your contemporary relationships.

Support Through Challenges

As you face non-public demanding conditions and uncertainties, your pals may be a precious supply of guide and encouragement. Lean on every one-of-a-kind eventually of those instances to beautify your bonds.

Celebrate Achievements

Celebrate each top notch's achievements and successes, irrespective of how massive or small. Recognizing the ones milestones continues your friendships colourful.

Tips for Handling Friendships Over Time

1. Open Communication: Maintain open and sincere communique together along with your buddies. Share your desires, disturbing conditions, and lifestyles transitions, and encourage them to do the identical.

2. Adaptability: Be flexible and adaptable for your friendships. Understand that adjustments will upward thrust up, and the capability to comply can keep your connections.

3. Prioritize Key Relationships: While you could have many buddies, prioritize key

friendships that maintain special this means that that to you.

4. Plan Reunions: When possible, plan reunions or get-togethers with friends who are now at a distance. These gatherings can reignite your connection.

five. Embrace New Interests Together: Explore new pursuits and passions together, as this may create new shared reports and hold your friendships thrilling.

6. Maintain Mutual Respect: Continue to admire every unique's selections, notwithstanding the fact that they create approximately precise paths. Mutual apprehend is the cornerstone of lasting friendships.

10.3 Conflict Resolution and Difficult Conversations

Navigating the Rough Waters

Friendships are not constantly easy crusing. Challenges and conflicts are a part of any dating. Learning to navigate those tough waters is important for maintaining and nurturing friendships.

Addressing Conflict

When conflicts rise up, it is important to cope with them in place of avoid or suppress them. Addressing issues head-on lets in for choice and boom within the friendship.

Active Listening

Practice energetic listening in the route of hard conversations. Give your pals the possibility to explicit their mind and feelings, and certainly be aware of their mindset.

Empathy

Empathy is a powerful device for resolving conflicts. Try to peer the situation from your pal's factor of view and validate their emotions.

Constructive Communication

Use optimistic communique to unique your private feelings and troubles. Be clear and respectful on your discussions and keep away from blame or hostility.

Finding Common Ground

Seek not unusual ground and solutions that gain every parties. Compromise is regularly crucial in war resolution.

Apologizing and Forgiving

When you've got made a mistake or have damage your buddy, do not hesitate to apologize in reality. On the flip component, be forgiving at the same time as your pals make errors.

Learn and Grow

Conflict can be an opportunity for growth and facts. Use it as a danger to take a look at more about your friends and your very very own strengths and weaknesses.

Tips for Conflict Resolution and Difficult Conversations

1. Choose the Right Time and Place: Ensure you have got got a suitable environment for discussing tough topics, in which you can communicate with out distractions or interruptions.

2. Stay Calm: Keep your feelings in check throughout difficult conversations. Emotional reactions can give a boost to conflicts, making choice more tough.

3. Use "I" Statements: Express your emotions the usage of "I" statements to keep away from putting blame to your pals. For instance, say, "I felt harm even as..." in choice to "You damage me even as..."

4. Avoid Accusations: Avoid making accusations or using aggressive language. Focus on the issue reachable in location of attacking your friend in my view.

five. Seek Mediation: If conflicts persist and are tough to remedy to your very non-public, remember in search of the assist of a relied on friend or mentor to mediate the verbal exchange.

6. Accept Differences: Recognize that variations in evaluations, values, and possibilities are herbal in friendships. Embrace the ones variations, as they may be capable of beautify your connections.

7. Reflect on Solutions: Take time to reflect on feasible answers and compromises in advance than project hard conversations.

Handling conflicts and difficult conversations with grace and maturity is a ability that might help your friendships. It permits you to assemble a foundation of accept as actual with and knowledge for you to serve your relationships properly as they evolve over the years.

www.ingramcontent.com/pod-product-compliance
Lightning Source LLC
Chambersburg PA
CBHW071443080526
44587CB00014B/1964